"Debra Burris has written the definitive book where myth, weather, and science are beautifully woven into an enjoyable and cohesive tapestry. With clear explanations and easy-to-do exercises, *Weather Magic* is an invitation to the expert or novice to explore the possibilities that weather energy can lend to your magical practice."

—**RAINA STARR,** host/producer of *Desperate House Witches*

"Debra Burris is both a physicist and witch, and she gives us a clear picture of what is actually going on in the atmosphere to cause weather, then weaves that knowledge into magical workings that are both useful and imaginative…. This book is about working with the weather in ways that empower our witchcraft and strengthen our ties to the planet and its web of life."

—**DIOTIMA MANTINEIA,** astrologer, soil/crop scientist, and author
  of *Touch the Earth, Kiss the Sky*

"Debra Burris reminds us of the beauty and magic of a raindrop and a rainbow. And then she takes us further by giving us spells and charms to work weather magic. Her words brought to me a way to understand weather formation that I never experienced before. The weather and magical descriptions are easy to understand and apply personally to my life."

—**MARLA K. ROBERSON,** Georgian Elder and High Priestess,
  programming director of Mystic South Conference

"Debra Burris has deftly interwoven her magickal practices with her professional training as an astrophysicist. The striking result is *Weather Magic*, a deep dive into the physics of weather phenomena and the methods practitioners of magick might employ to better align their energies with the meteorological elements around them. Accessible and authoritatively written, *Weather Magic* offers readers multiple tips and tricks to sharpen their awareness of and deepen their connections with the abundant natural magic of Earth."

—**MARTHA KIRBY CAPO,** coauthor of *Thrifty Witchery*

"If you've ever thought science and magic can't possibly coexist, Debra Burris is about to show you otherwise in *Weather Magic.…* Her rich knowledge of science and natural phenomena shines through, and the end result is a compendium of powerful weather magic, complete with exercises, rituals, and small daily practices to get your workings off the ground."

—**PATTI WIGINGTON,** author of *Witchcraft for Healing, Badass Ancestors,* and *The Witch's Complete Guide to Tarot*

WEATHER MAGIC

WITCHERY, SCIENCE, LORE

ABOUT THE AUTHOR

Debra L. Burris, PhD, professor of physics and astronomy, researches the wondrous phenomena of stellar evolution, focusing on the astrophysical origins of the star dust of which we are all made. She also has guided student research into storm formation and the charging mechanism of thunderstorms that creates lightning.

Debra is an elder in the Georgian Tradition of Wicca as well as a practitioner of her own version of Ozark Mountain Witchery, focusing on weather magic, working with bones, and using native plants. Her personal gnosis is searching for the connections between her love of science and her spiritual practice, reveling in the mystery and wonder of both and how they are branches of the same tree. These connections are the focus of her writing and presentations at conferences across the South, including United Earth Assembly, Sacred Journey, Prairie Meet, Enchanted Metaphysical & Mystics Market, and Mystic South. Recently her work has turned toward healing her ancestral wounds, working to undo the damage of colonizing ancestors. Remembering we are all someone's ancestor, she is working to move away from these ancestral wounds of racism, homophobia, misogyny, and xenophobia toward an inclusive, just, and accepting path for her spiritual line.

A third-generation farmer, Debra raises cattle and horses. She is also a haven to a variety of rescue animals, including miniature horses and donkeys, dogs, and cats. The mission of Buckthorn Farms includes preserving heritage livestock breeds and homesteading skills. Even the farm is included in her spiritual work, as she explores being land tied and what her relationship with the land and farm means and how it can evolve in a healthy way. On her farm she has studied many hands-on skills, including canning, preserving, seed saving, plant allyship, sewing, knitting, and basketry. Her ultimate goal is to start an educational nonprofit supporting these ideals at her farm. You can hear about all her adventures on her YouTube podcast, *Diary of a Physicist Farmgal*.

WEATHER MAGIC

WITCHERY, SCIENCE, LORE

DEBRA L. BURRIS

LLEWELLYN PUBLICATIONS
Woodbury, Minnesota

First Edition
First Printing, 2024

Book design by R. Brasington
Cover design by Kevin R. Brown
Interior illustrations by Llewellyn Art Department

Llewellyn Publications is a registered trademark of Llewellyn Worldwide Ltd.

Library of Congress Cataloging-in-Publication Data (Pending)
ISBN: 978-0-7387-7579-1

Llewellyn Publications
A Division of Llewellyn Worldwide Ltd.
2143 Wooddale Drive
Woodbury, MN 55125-2989
www.llewellyn.com

Printed in the United States of America

Acknowledgments

I am blessed beyond measure to have a family of choice who encouraged me to pursue writing this book. Even when I doubted my ability to do this, they were there cheering me on.

Marla, Gypsey, and Stacy, for giving me the push I needed to pursue the idea.

Serendipity, for quite literally holding my hand as we waited to be brave little toasters to pitch our ideas.

Heather, for taking a chance on a green-as-grass newbie.

Raina, Dorothy, and Byron, for taking my messages and calls to answer my questions and give honest opinions.

Gina, for being my accountability partner.

Marla, Stacy, Krista, and Cassie, for giving me honest and supportive feedback as alpha readers.

My online crafting group—Penny, Tyra, Jessica, Shirley, Nancy, Sarah, Ashley, and Kirsty—for listening to me ramble on and reason out ideas for many, many hours.

Scott, Carol, Tim, Joel, and Rachel, for sharing personal experiences, being proud of me, and supporting me in my moments of insecurity.

All the organizers of events who took a chance on letting me teach and to everyone who has come out to support me at these events. And to my local community, for always supporting me and believing in me.

My heart is full. "All these simple dreams."

D. L. B.

Contents

EXERCISES AND ACTIVITIES

FOREWORD

Gypsey Elaine Teague

Growing up in New Hampshire, I knew when it was going to rain. I was taught by my grandfather how to tell if the snow would be deep and fluffy or heavy and wet. He showed me flowers that would warn you of incoming weather and usually which directions the weather was coming from. However, my grandfather and my other family members never told me why these things happened and what you could do to manipulate some of them.

Then came Debra Burris's book on weather magic. I truly wish I'd had this book while growing up and farming in New Hampshire, serving a number of years with the military going to the field almost every week, and experiencing both good and not-so-good weather throughout my elder years.

This book says it all. From cute sayings that actually have a lesson to teach to spells and incantations that will assist you through the year, Dr. Burris's book has it all. Debra speaks with a frankness and an authentic intelligence of one who knows this not just as a witch but as a scientist.

I have been to her farm. I've witnessed firsthand how what she knows affects what she does and how she does it better and with less effort or stress because of it. Her book is a compilation of her life and her experiences. I love the way she breaks everything down, gives you the science, gives you the magic, and then winds it up with a concise conclusion to each section that puts it all in context, which is essential in dealing with things not everyone knows or understands.

Since reading this book, I have begun using her chapters on our small holding, and the results have been exceptional. I cannot change the weather, but I can understand why the weather changes. Right now I'm in the middle of a massive thunderstorm. When I looked at the chapter on that, it gave me insight into which way the storm was going, how far away it was; it's not always as easy as counting after thunder to see how many miles away the lightning is and analyzing what kind of rain is coming down. Yes, there are different kinds of rain, just like there are different types of clouds. Something else I never knew.

Finally, it doesn't hurt that Debra is a close friend. I've seen her work her magic firsthand and how that knowledge has assisted her on her farm and in her life. Normally at this point, the reviewer says something like, "If you only buy one book…get this one," but there is *only* one book like *this*. So, this is obviously the one you want, not just because it's the only one, but because it's the definitive one. I feel there could be an entire shelf of similar books on the subject; there isn't, but this would still be the one you should purchase.

As the writer of this albeit short foreword, I am expected to write great things about the book, give a glowing review, tell you how wonderful your life would be if you purchased it, and what it would mean to me if you did. All these things I do not because

I was asked to write this—I wasn't—but because I believe in what I've said; *I* was the one who asked to write this. I thought it needed to be said.

I hope Debra writes more books on magic, but I doubt she will ever be able to write a better weather magic book than this one.

Gypsey Elaine Teague

Author of

Norse Divination

A Witch's Guide to Wands

Steampunk Magic

INTRODUCTION

I spent many summer days in the hayfield as a child. I would lie on the trailer in the shade of a big oak tree and stare up at the fluffy cumulus clouds, seeing dragons, horses, fairies, and other fantastical beings. I watched them billow into the sky and imagined being carried up by them. I watched the rain fall out of them and thought that was a gateway for spirits to travel down to Earth. Then the grown-up world came crashing in to tell me to stop wasting my time on childish things. I stopped looking up.

The sky once again enchanted me when I began to learn the science behind it in my high school Earth Science class. The physics behind the energy of weather explained how clouds and storms formed, how energy changed to manifest rain or snow or sometimes a tornado. This fascination followed me into college and even into graduate school where I took courses with meteorology students. I learned the patterns of energy that created weather and learned that weather will share its secrets if you just pay attention.

As I worked on my doctorate in physics, I was gaining knowledge in astrophysics and how the elements we are made of come from the cosmos, so we are connected to the universe. At the same time, I was spreading my wings in my spiritual studies. Soon I started to see places where there was commonality in ideas and even overlap in my spiritual and scientific studies. I began to understand they were interconnected, and that, to me, made them even more powerful.

Today, as a physicist and a witch, I refuse to separate my science from my magic. I think they are two sides of the same energetic coin and work in harmony. By understanding the physics of weather, I can find sources of energy that I never considered before. So, why not use the physics of weather to inform my magical practice?

What Is Weather Magic?

When people think about weather magic, they often think of someone trying to control the weather, like magical versions of the Rainmaker.[1] This is one way to work with weather energy that draws a lot of ire and fear. People don't like the idea of changing the weather, because it goes against their idea of the universe having a reason for everything. Yet, they have no issue doing energy work for a new job or a new love or to sell their home. I propose that working with weather is the same. Likely most of us have tried it in that way even if we don't really acknowledge it. How many times as a kid did I chant "rain, rain, go away" or wait with bated breath, fingers crossed with hope in my heart, as the list of school closings scrolled by on the early morning newscast? That, my friends, is weather magic!

1. Anthony, *Rainmaker*, 1956.

We have protection and preparation rituals we go through when a storm is headed our way. We just call this "getting ready" or "well, I just stuck that knife in the ground like granny used to." We pray the storm isn't as bad or that it passes us by. We pray for rain in dry times, to put out fires, to help crops grow, to cool off a heat wave. We hope it doesn't rain on our wedding day or on an outdoor concert we have been waiting to see. When we wish that the rain holds off until we get to our car or when we wish on a rainbow, we are doing weather magic. Every time we plant a garden and hope that the conditions are right for it to flourish, we are doing weather magic. It may seem like these are just mundane thoughts, but we are using those thoughts to manipulate energy to our desire outcome. That is weather magic—simple weather magic.

Some aspects of weather magic are more difficult. This type of work, when taken on with intention, should be done by those with experience and knowledge of how to properly ground, center, and protect themselves. I learned a great phrase in a study group I was in: *energy hygiene*. When you send out energetic tendrils to connect with others, with the energy of the earth or the universe or Spirit, you need to remember to bring those tendrils back when you are done with the working. You can't leave those energetic connections marooned out there with no intent or purpose. Don't let yourself remain open energetically when the work is finished. That is true with weather magic and why I advise working with an experienced energy practitioner at first. These are big energies; they don't need to be left untethered or unattended.

There are works someone new to magic can do safely, such as protection work for your home and family, learning to do cloud divination, or using weather map symbols for sigils or as a type of "rune." Always seek counsel and ask questions from trusted mentors, energy workers, and magical practitioners if you aren't sure. We all started in the same place, and most every practitioner, witch, or energy worker I know is willing to talk to those who have a sincere interest in learning.

APPROACHING WEATHER MAGIC

Magic, energy work, or whatever label feels right to you is much like a game of chess in my way of thinking. You have to think several moves ahead to really see the full impact of what you are setting into motion, regardless of what your direct intention is. Then you have to decide if those ramifications are ones you can live with. At the end of the day, you are accountable for your work, regardless of what path you follow. Owning that accountability is part of being a practitioner or an energy worker.

No magic exists in a bubble. We do work for a new job; that may mean someone is fired or someone didn't get the job over us. We do work for rain; that may mean it rains on someone else's parade, quite literally. Physics tells us that every action has a reaction. My advice is to understand that there is going to be an impact beyond yourself and your intent. Sometimes, you just need to get stuff done! Sometimes, you may decide another way would be better.

These decisions are why working with these big energies is best done once you have some experience, education, and self-reflection under your belt. Understanding implications, responsibilities, and the long-term impact of your work is something that comes from doing work on yourself first. It's not fun, but trust me, it's worth the effort in the long run. As a witch, I am at my best and most effective when I am right within myself. Isn't that what we all learned when we first started on this path? We need to remember those first principles, and we need to remember we are ultimately accountable for whatever intention and impact we put out into the universe.

If you don't feel comfortable working with the energy of weather in this sense yet, that is perfectly okay. There is a myriad of good resources out there for you to build up your abilities, discernment, and confidence. These resources give advice on how to practice basic magic responsibly, in a healthy and safe way. That doesn't mean that understanding weather and working with it in some way are not for you.

MY WEATHER MAGIC PRACTICE

I often get a strange response from people when I talk about working with weather in my practice. They seem surprised that I would even think of using weather. It's as if it never occurred to them that weather is part of what Mother Nature offers us. They have no issues learning plants, stones, or even the directions and all the associated correspondences. They look at the sky to study the stars and planets. Somehow the idea that weather is also there waiting for us is not even on the radar, pun intended.

While I am an Elder in the Georgian Tradition of Witchcraft, my personal practice has evolved into something much more land tied. When I started reading Nathan M. Hall's book *Path of the Moonlit Hedge*, I saw that many of my beliefs fall under Animism.[2] I see the land I live on, the trees, the clouds, the river, the rock, the animals, the flowers all flowing with Spirit. This Spirit suffuses everything in my world, and I use this energy in my magical practice. As a witch, I regularly draw on the energy of the earth and of the elements.

In this sense, I work with weather energy, not to try to manipulate the weather necessarily, but to tap into the energy weather possesses. Weather is an amazing source of energy that is right

---

2. Hall, *Path of the Moonlit Hedge*, 9.

outside my door, so why shouldn't I draw on that energy for work I want to do? It is the same energy, just packaged differently. In her book *Weather or Not*, author Katrina Rasbold beautifully described working with the energy of weather as "our working partner."[3]

I have the privilege of living up close and personal with Mother Nature here on my Ozark foothills farm. Weather is very much a partner in my day-to-day life here. Its impact cannot be denied. Trying to fight against it is a fruitless pursuit. I have to learn to work with it as a partner if I want my farm to survive and prosper. Learning to read the skies allows me to be as prepared as I can for whatever is on the way. Seeing weather's awesome impact led me to think more deeply about how I can use it in my magical practice.

Some of you may not live in an area where Mother Nature is easily accessible. Maybe you don't live in an area that routinely gets certain types of weather. That's okay! Whatever path you follow, energy shows up as part of that practice at some point. Because energy is part of weather, it is accessible without any special tools. You can work with the energies directly, using the tools nature provides: the rain, the wind, the sunlight. These are all part of weather energy.

It is my hope that by understanding the science of weather and how it ties into the lore, you can adapt what you learn to your own practice. I will try to give you a few ideas about how you can incorporate things you don't normally get to experience in your practice. For example, if you don't live in area that sees snowfall, maybe you can make your own on a smaller scale like some of us did in school with paper and scissors.

---

3. Rasbold, *Weather or Not*, 5.

My Goal Is to Inspire

The goal I have for this book is to give you some insight into the physics of weather systems to, I hope, inspire you to fold these ideas into your personal magical practice. While I plan to share examples of what I do, these are not meant to be prescriptive. In my experience, the best magic is personal and intuitive, so my suggestions are only meant to give you some ideas. There is freedom in understanding how the energy of weather works. You can then tailor it to suit your needs and the needs of your community. You have the agency to find what works best for you!

More than anything else, I hope this book inspires you to reclaim that childlike wonder and awe of the weather. I hope you can rekindle that connection to your sense of amazement, and to nature. Remember who you were before the world crashed in and said, "Stop acting like a child looking at clouds." Remember, you are allowed to choose your magical path. Most importantly, look up!

Chapter 1
BACK TO BASICS

What is weather? It is the short-term condition of the atmosphere at a particular location. It is not the same as climate, which is a long-term average condition at a location. Let's clear that up right out of the gate. What is the starting point for all weather phenomena? The three necessary ingredients are the sun, the atmosphere, and water.

THE SUN

Our sun, approximately ninety-three million miles away, is Earth's primary source of heating. Because of the type of star the sun is, it emits most of its radiant energy in the form of visible light, but it also emits significant amounts of infrared (IR) and ultraviolet (UV) light and much smaller amounts of other wavelengths of light. IR light is what we normally think of as heat: the warmth of a fire, the heat from a hot skillet, body heat. It is simply another form of light energy, just one our eye is not sensitive to. The absorption of

IR by the water vapor in our atmosphere is a major piece of the weather puzzle.

Some forms of light are highly energetic, like UV, X-rays, and gamma rays. It isn't healthy to be overexposed to those. That is why X-ray techs leave the room or get behind a shield of some kind while they are taking the image. Ultraviolet is what we guard against when we wear sunscreen, since prolonged exposure can cause skin cancer. Gamma rays are both a form of electromagnetic (EM) radiation and a product of radioactive decay, but we are generally safe from exposure to those. In some cases, gamma rays can be very useful, such as in positron-emission tomography (PET) scans or in some forms of cancer treatments.

We will focus mainly on IR and visible light, with a bit on UV. Visible and IR light are the main driving forces of weather.

Visible sunlight is composed of all the colors of the spectrum. You may have learned the mnemonic *ROYGBIV* to represent the colors: red, orange, yellow, green, blue, indigo, violet. Even though our sun peaks in the green part of the spectrum, sunlight contains all the ROYGBIV colors. I like to use sunlight to charge tools, jewelry, altar items, and spell components.

EXERCISE
Charging Magical Items with Sunlight

Using sunlight is a good way to charge and cleanse magical items. I want to challenge you to try seeing the sunlight as its component colors and using that knowledge to charge items for specific purposes.

Some color associations I often use:

Red: romantic love, passion, creative energy

Orange: familial or platonic love, expansion, transformation

Yellow: happiness, joy, motivation

Green: wealth, prosperity, growth

Blue: healing, peace, comfort and consolation

Indigo: learning, self-expression, deep understanding

Violet: spiritual growth, manifestation, cosmic connection

You will need

- the magical items you want to charge
- a sunny location
- colored transparent plastic for filtering (if desired)
- a way to secure the plastic if working outside

Directions

Try to time this spell for midday. When the sun is directly overhead, you get less scattering of light since it travels through less of the atmosphere than it does at sunrise or sunset, so you are getting maximum benefit from the light.

Choose a location that gets direct sunlight for at least a couple of hours. Make sure your items will be secure and will be able to tolerate direct sunlight. Candles, for example, might not fare well on a summer afternoon!

If you want to focus on a particular color, choose a transparent plastic in that color and lay it over the item. Be sure to secure it if you are working outdoors. I often use colored plastic wrap or those plastic report covers we all used in high school. If you prefer to use all the colors, the filter isn't necessary.

After you have arranged your items, spend time visualizing the sunlight bathing them in its energy. If you wish, you also can imagine it imbuing them with UV or IR energy to add a little extra boost to the charging. You could also visualize the different properties of the layers of the atmosphere being added to the sunlight as it travels, if those are elements you want to add to the charging. Try to move beyond just seeing it as simple sunlight, instead adding all the extra benefits to the richness of the energy it gives your items.

Leave the items in the sunlight for as long as they are receiving direct light or at least for a couple of hours. Then remove them from the spot; be sure to not leave behind any plastic filters.

If you won't have access to a sunny spot, a good alternative is to use a natural sunlight lightbulb, or if that is not available, bright indirect sunlight would do. If you opt for indirect sunlight, I suggest leaving the items in it for as long as possible since you aren't getting the intensity of light directly from the sun. Otherwise, I would follow the procedure as described.

To extend this exercise, you could think about the way colors combine in light. They are additive colors, unlike when mixing pigments, which is subtractive color. The primary colors of light are red, green, and blue. These colors combine to give us the secondary colors. The secondary colors are yellow (red plus green), magenta (red plus blue), and cyan (green plus blue). There are also complementary colors that, when mixed, give white light. The complementary pairings are red-cyan, blue-yellow, and green-magenta. You could use this knowledge to get very specific with your color selection for your item charging.

THE ATMOSPHERE

Our atmosphere has evolved over the life of the planet, but at present, it is mostly nitrogen and oxygen, with smaller amounts of water vapor and carbon dioxide. It extends upward for dozens of miles and it gets thinner the higher you go. The thickest layer is the one we live in, the troposphere. The troposphere is where the vast majority of weather events take place. Generally, as you rise in the troposphere, the temperatures will cool. A good rule of thumb is about 3.5 degrees Fahrenheit (2 degrees Celsius) for every increase of 1000 feet in altitude.

Troposphere

Once you get to the top of the troposphere, there is a layer where there is very little temperature change as altitude increases. The tropopause is where the jet streams reside, so there are strong horizontal winds in this layer. We'll see later that this is the layer that cuts off the tops of the cumulonimbus clouds, giving them their distinctive anvil tops.

The altitude of the troposphere decreases with latitude. The troposphere is at its highest altitude near the equator, meaning that is where the troposphere is the thickest. As you move toward the poles, the altitude of the tropopause decreases. There is also a seasonal variation in the thickness of the troposphere. The location of the tropopause is overall higher in the summer months than it is in the winter.

Stratosphere

The stratosphere is the next layer. It gets its name from the stratification of the temperature layers in it. The stratosphere is home to the ozone layer, and the ozone layer is what is responsible for temperature changes. While the troposphere cools as you rise in altitude, the stratosphere has a temperature inversion, so it increases in temperature as you climb.

Let's take a minute to talk about what temperature means in a science sense. We think of temperature as a way to feel how hot or cold something is. At our location in the atmosphere, that is a by-product of temperature to be sure. Temperature from a thermodynamic perspective is the measure of the energy of moving particles: kinetic energy. It doesn't matter if there is one particle or many; the more active they are, the higher the temperature. What we perceive is due to the interactions of huge numbers of these air molecules with our skin. The more active they are, the more interactions or collisions, and we say that is hot. Low-activity particles won't interact as much, so we say that is cold. But if we went to an area of the atmosphere where the density is much lower, we wouldn't feel hot, even if the molecules had lots of energy. This is because of the low number of interactions.

So, the question remains: How does the ozone layer cause the temperature of the stratosphere to increase so rapidly? Ozone is a molecule composed of three oxygen atoms. It is a very efficient absorber of UV light. You may hear about "ozone alert" days when the air quality is poor. Ozone in the troposphere is problematic, but in the stratosphere, it is vitally important. It acts as the earth's sunscreen. The energy of the absorption causes the molecule to break apart, but it reforms, releasing even more energy. All this energy in the molecules causes their temperature to rise dramatically.

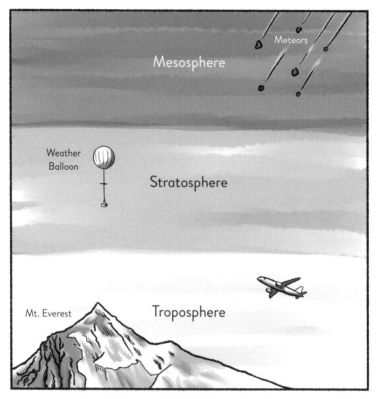

Figure 1: Earth's Atmosphere

Very little weather occurs in the stratosphere, but there are some clouds that form near the poles. The stratosphere has very little moisture, but during the polar winters, these icy clouds can form. These clouds are sometimes called nacreous, or mother-of-pearl, clouds due to their iridescent appearance. There are also some electrical phenomena associated with strong thunderstorms that appear in the stratosphere. These are called jets and sprites. They aren't well understood and are still a subject of much scientific study.

Mesosphere

The next layer is the mesosphere. In this layer, 99.9 percent of the mass of the atmosphere is beneath you. The air temperature in the mesosphere decreases again as altitude increases. In fact, the top of the mesosphere is the coldest part of Earth's atmosphere. There can be some very high thin clouds here called noctilucent clouds. These are also usually found near the poles and are so thin they are only visible during twilight. This layer is where many of the meteors that enter Earth's atmosphere burn up and are visible to us as shooting stars.

Above the mesosphere is the thermosphere, and as its name implies, the molecules here are very energetic, so we would say they have a high temperature. They get this energy when the oxygen in this layer absorbs energy from the solar wind. Above this is the exosphere, where the particles have enough energy to escape Earth's gravitational pull and are able to stream off into space. I will focus on the troposphere since that is where the majority of weather takes place.

EXERCISE
Atmosphere Climb Visualization

Here is a simple visualization exercise to try. The goal of this visualization is to build up energy then release it to work on a specific target or goal. If possible, go outside and sit in the sunshine. If not, try to imagine the sunlight bathing your skin.

You will need
- nothing but yourself

Directions

Whether you are outside or inside, sit down comfortably and close your eyes. If you are outside, notice how the sunlight warms your skin and allow this warmth to soak into your being. If you are inside, imagine this same warmth.

Feel the energy coursing through you, building up the energy you will eventually send on its way. Focus on your purpose for this energy. Is it healing? Is it protection? The lovely thing about sunlight is it contains all the colors of the rainbow, so you can filter the color you want if you wish, or you can use all the colors if you choose.

When you are satisfied with the energy you have built up, imagine yourself rising upward through the troposphere. Notice the air around you cooling, the breezes washing over you. As you continue to rise to cooler air, imagine the energy you stored working its way to the outer layers of your skin, moving to your hands. The more the air around you cools, feel the energy "ball" growing stronger. Focus on drawing all the energy you gathered from the sunlight into the ball, letting it strengthen until you are ready to send it out.

Open your hands, directing the released energy to flow to its destination. See it as a colorful ribbon of light extending off to your desired recipient. Once you have completed your energy sending, visualize yourself floating gently downward to the ground again. Feel the air around you warming as you descend. Once you have returned to the ground, you should make sure to ground and center yourself, then perform any energy working aftercare you would normally do.

EXERCISE
Aeromancy

Aeromancy is divination using the general conditions of the atmosphere. One form of historical aeromancy that even the most reserved person may partake in is the tradition of Groundhog Day. Cloudy days mean no shadow, so a shorter winter. There are many historical variations of this tradition, including the weather conditions on Imbolc or Candlemas. There are many directions this could go—studying the clouds, the winds, or even things like meteors.

Here is a simple exercise you can try.

You will need
- an even number of paper slips
- a container to hold the slips
- a writing utensil

Directions
Find a location outdoors, preferably protected from the breeze. Think of a question that has a yes-no answer. As you are focusing on the question, write *yes* on half the slips of paper, *no* on the other half. Place your slips in the container. I usually don't fold them, but you can. At your breeze-free location, dump the slips out of the bowl from a height and allow them to float to the ground. The first paper to reach the ground gives your answer.

As an extension to this exercise, you could use aeromancy to make predictions about the upcoming year. Historically, a form of aeromancy practiced in Greece, *Minallagia*, focuses on weather and atmospheric conditions, particularly in the month of August.[4] Conditions on particular days predict the weather for its associated month of the coming year. This is similar to the liturgical traditions of the Ember Days as observed in Spain. In some traditions, the direction of the wind on the Ember Days predicts the weather for the coming year.

EXERCISE
Omen Days Divination

For this exercise, consider Omen Days, the days from December 26 to January 6.[5] In Celtic folklore, the atmospheric conditions on these days, as well as nature observations and divination or oracular work, predicted the weather for each month of the coming year.

You will need
- a calendar
- a notebook and writing instrument
- preferred divination tool(s)
- weather app (optional)

Directions
You will do this work daily for twelve days. In your notebook, label a page for each day and the corresponding month. Observe the weather conditions throughout the day and record. If desired, perform divination each day and record that as well. How you choose to do this divination is entirely up to you. It can be a one-card pull from

---

4. Kokkinos, *Occupied Towns/Displaced Municipalities of the Republic of Cyprus*, 39.

5. Gwyndaf, "Welsh Tradition-Bearers," 77–91.

a tarot or oracle deck; it can be a rune you have drawn; it can be an elaborate spread from multiple sources. It is all about what you feel drawn to do. I also pay special attention to animal sightings, events, or my general mood that day as part of my observations.

At the beginning of each month for the following year, review your recorded notes as insights for the month ahead. At the end of the month, go back and review them again to note how well the events of the month lined up with your Omen Days predictions.

One thing I try to do each month is add notes to areas I felt were particularly useful or accurate in my divination work. I also take a photo of my divination spread and add that to my notebook to easily refer to each month.

WATER

Energy arrives from the sun to our blue planet, where some gets absorbed by the water vapor in the earth's atmosphere. The various surfaces on the earth also absorb some of it: the ocean, land, concrete, and so on. All these different materials have different specific heat capacities. For example, sand absorbs and releases heat quicker than water because it has a lower specific heat capacity. Water has one of the highest specific heat capacities of the things we will talk about. In the case of a balanced energy budget, eventually this energy gets released back into space and the overall average temperature of the planet stays constant. Climate change is obviously affecting this, but we won't discuss that here other than to acknowledge that it is a very real and present danger to our planet.

Water vapor is the key to the energy needed for weather to happen. Water vapor is the gaseous form of water. It can be formed by boiling or evaporating water. It can also be formed in the right conditions by the sublimation of ice. We will talk more about these processes shortly.

The amount of water vapor in the atmosphere varies over time and by location. Water vapor is fantastic at storing heat energy. In technical terms, we say it has a high specific heat capacity. Basically, that means water holds on to heat very well. The old adage "a watched pot never boils" comes from the fact that it seemingly takes a long time to heat up water. The flip side of this is once that heat is stored in the water, it takes an equally long time to release it. This is why coastal regions tend to be more temperate than inland areas of the same latitude. That release of energy is what drives most weather phenomena.

The released energy is what is used to drive weather, so it is important to understand how this happens. How does water vapor release this energy? There are two ways. The first is cooling, the second is changing phases. Mathematically, it can be complicated to understand these processes, but conceptually, we see them right in our own homes.

Revisiting the boiling pot of water, the reason the water boils is it has been on the stove where heat has been added over time. I say the pot "heats up," and that shows up as the temperature rising. Now let's say I turn off the stove, so I stop adding heat to the pot. What happens? The water in the pot starts to release this heat put in it over time. From a science standpoint, what is happening is the water is trying to come into temperature equilibrium with its surroundings by releasing its heat. It will release heat until it comes back down to the same temperature as its surroundings. In physics, this process of moving heat around is called thermodynamics. In a very broad sense, everything in the universe is trying to come into equilibrium with everything else. This means heat is always on the move.

How Heat Moves

What happens to the water if I continue to add heat to the pot? I notice bubbles forming at the bottom of the pot. These bubbles will rise to surface of the water and burst. I also notice steam coming off the surface of the water. In this simple example, there are two thermodynamic processes that create weather: convection and phase change.

The bubbles are the process of convection. Most people are familiar with the idea that hot air rises. It turns out, so does hot water. Convection is a way that fluids can move heat around.

Think about watching a thunderstorm seem to boil up as it forms. It is using convection to carry energy upward into the atmosphere. This convection releases energy into the upper parts of the storm, and this is the fuel it needs to continue.

Phase Changes

Another weather process is modeling the second part of the boiling pot: the steam. Water has three forms, or phases: solid (ice), liquid, and gas (steam). What is needed for water to transform from one phase to another? The steam forms because the heat the water is taking on eventually raises its temperature to its boiling point. If I keep adding heat, something else has to happen; there is a limit to the amount of heat liquid water can take on.

The additional heat changes the form of the water from liquid to gas. During this process, the temperature of water doesn't change. All the energy goes into changing the phase of the water. The steam formed will be the same temperature as the liquid water right after it forms. Phase changes contain a lot of heat energy. In fact, the phase change from liquid water to steam contains more heat than the change from the freezing point to the boiling point. That is why steam scalds are so severe. The heat that causes the phase change is called latent heat. *Latent* means "hidden" in this context. The reason it is called latent is that there isn't any temperature change when the phase change is happening. Latent heat of fusion is the heat involved in a solid-to-liquid or liquid-to-solid phase change. Latent heat of vaporization is responsible for a liquid-to-gas or gas-to-liquid phase change.

Evaporation is also a phase change from liquid to gas, but it occurs below the boiling point. It occurs from the surface of water when molecules get enough energy to escape the water. How rapidly evaporation happens depends on several factors, including air temperature, wind speed, humidity, and if the sun is shining. Evaporation from large bodies of water or from vegetation is what provides humidity to the air.

There is one other form of phase change that sometimes occurs, although it is rarer. Sometimes conditions allow for solids to go directly into gas or gas to deposit directly into solids. If you have ever used dry ice for a smoke effect, you have seen this in action. The dry ice is the solid form of carbon dioxide. It is called "dry" because it doesn't go through a liquid phase; instead, it goes directly from solid to gas. This process is called sublimation. It is also a phase change and has its own value of latent heat. Occasionally, the conditions can exist where water ice can sublimate directly to water vapor.

The water vapor rising in the atmosphere to create clouds and storms uses phase change energy. When you look at a cloud, you might notice dark gray areas at the base and bright whiter areas higher up. The dark areas are the parts that contain the liquid water that has condensed from the water vapor. The bright white areas contain ice that has frozen from the liquid water. The cooling and freezing release all that energy that is stored in the water vapor.

I work with this phase change energy to think about a situation I might want to solidify, like liquid transferring to ice, or to dispel, like liquid becoming vapor.

EXERCISE
Ice Cube Spell

Try this simple phase change spell using an ice cube. There are two versions of this spell: to warm up a situation and let things flow, or to cool down and solidify a situation.

For a warming flow, you will need
- a frozen ice cube
- a slip of paper
- a permanent marker
- a pin or needle
- a dish or saucer to catch the water

Warming flow directions
Think of a word or two that pertain to the situation you want to create flow in. Is there something blocking this flow? Think of a word that identifies that block. Write the words on the slip of paper. I like to use a permanent marker for this so it doesn't get diluted by the melting water. Use a pin or needle or something with a sharp point; carefully scribe the word you associate with the

energy block on the ice cube. Place the slip of paper in the dish, then set the ice cube on top.

For a little added energy, you could place the dish in the sunlight to let its energy help the melting of the ice cube. As the ice cube melts, visualize the block to your situation melting along with it. As the water collects on the paper, visualize the energy in that liquid water flowing into the situation that your piece of paper represents.

Let the cube melt completely, allowing all the energy you visualized pour into the situation you want to see flow in. Dispose of the water on a potted plant or a plant outside, then let the paper dry out in the sunshine. Keep the paper where you can go back to it and watch the results of your warming spell take shape. Once you have gotten your desired result, dispose of the paper to release any excess energy that might be left behind back into the atmosphere.

To solidify a situation, you will need

- water
- an ice cube tray
- a slip of paper
- a permanent marker

Solidify spell directions

You can do this work at any time. Think of a situation you want to solidify or cool off. Write a couple of words on the slip of paper in permanent marker. Place the slip in one of the slots on the ice cube tray, fill the tray with water, and place it in the freezer.

Visualize the ice cube forming around the paper, giving stability to the situation you are working for. Keep the cube frozen until the situation has resolved. Once you have achieved your goal, dispose of the ice cube, releasing any excess energy back into the atmosphere.

Option

If you aren't in a position to easily freeze or melt ice cubes, you could use a similar visualization of the energy. You could draw a map for the phase change with the words describing the situation you want to affect written inside the map. For a melting phase change, the first picture would be a drawing of a square or cube representing the ice cube, then the second picture would be a puddle shape. If you instead wanted to have a solidifying effect, you would simply reverse the order of the pictures.

EXERCISE
Boiling Water Spell

Maybe you have a situation you want to really pump some energy into. Try this exercise.

You will need
- a pot of water
- a wooden spoon
- food coloring (optional)

Directions

Place a pot of water on your stove. As you are waiting on it to come to boil, focus your intention on the desired outcome of your spell work. Think of one or two words that embody your intention. If there is a color that would enhance your spell (for example, green for a healing spell), add that now.

Using the wooden spoon, gently stir the water three times clockwise to build up the energy for your intention. Write the words three times in the water using the wooden spoon.

As the water begins to boil, imagine your intention and the energy of the water being carried away toward your intended recipient.

Note that if you don't have access to a stove, an alternative is to perform the same work and let the water evaporate over time. The effect will be the same; it will just act over a slower timeline.

Boiling Water Spell Extension

An extension of the boiling water spell is to carefully use the steam rising from the pot to cleanse tools or even your hands or face. This adds the energy of the work to whatever you have cleansed as well. Just be very careful that the steam isn't too hot. I will use this technique often in the winter when my skin or nose is dry and could benefit from the steam. You get magical work done and a nice pore cleanse or moisture bath at the same time. It's a win-win!

WEATHER LORE

The sun and atmosphere are the driving forces of our planet's weather. They also have been a source of fascination for humans from the very beginning. Stories about the sun and what goes on in the sky are ubiquitous, crossing all cultural boundaries. Weather has been the subject of folklore since it is key to the survival of crops and livestock. Even though fewer folks farm these days, understanding how the folklore foretells the weather can make life easier.

When the sun draws water, rain will follow.

My grandpa often said this one. We have all likely seen the rays of sunlight beaming through openings in a mostly overcast sky. These are called crepuscular rays. They are created by light scattering off the cloud forms. They can also be caused by light scattering off haze or dust at sunrise or sunset. Although these rays are often associated with partly or mostly cloudy conditions that can produce rain, there is no connection between the rays and any chance of rain.

If it rains when the sun shines,
it will surely rain again tomorrow about the same hour.

This was another of my grandpa's favorites. There are several variations of sayings regarding sun-showers (rain showers when the sun is also visible).

If it rains while the sun is shining,
the witches are making butter.

This is my personal favorite. I mean, who knew there was an official butter churning time? There really isn't any strong correlation to science in any of these sayings other than showery days mean there is a generally unstable pattern in place. With that pattern in place, there could be rain the next day, but it's certainly not guaranteed. I do really like the idea of witches making butter, so maybe I need to invest in a churn.

A more reliable indicator of weather can be found in the chirping of crickets. Because crickets use muscle contractions to create sound, they can do this more easily in warmer weather, so they chirp more frequently at higher temperatures. In fact, there is a formula for this known as Dolbear's law, named for Amos Dolbear, who published an article about this relationship in 1897.[6] Count the number of cricket chirps in fourteen seconds, then add forty to get the temperature in Fahrenheit.

WINDING IT UP

The sun and the earth's atmosphere are the driving forces behind weather. The process of sunlight traveling across space then through the multiple layers of the atmosphere brings energy to our planet. As a scientist, I see that energy as the source for all these different processes, from cloud formation to snowflake structure. As a farmer, I see the sun and the atmosphere as my partners for success in my agricultural endeavors. As a witch, I see all the potential magic in the energetic interplay of the sun and the atmosphere.

Now that you have a clearer understanding of the earth's atmosphere and all the forms of energy contained within it, I hope you are already thinking of ways you can include it in your practice. Can you think of another simple spell you could do with that phase change? What about using the light from the sun in more expansive ways? All that good juicy energy is all around us. Once you start thinking about the energy this way, even more new ideas will come to you!

6. Berenbaum, *Earwig's Tail*, 109–111.

Chapter 2
BLOWING IN THE WIND

The best place to begin our journey in the troposphere is with the big picture of global wind patterns. The earth's surface is unevenly heated by the sun for multiple reasons: the earth is tilted on its axis by 23.5 degrees, it has a variety of surfaces that absorb heat differently, and it has day and night. This uneven heating is the first piece of developing these global wind circulation cells.

These global winds are responsible to some degree for all weather on the planet. They connect us directly to the energy of both the sun and the ocean. They act over large distances and can be useful for long-range work. Understanding how and why the wind blows makes my magic more effective.

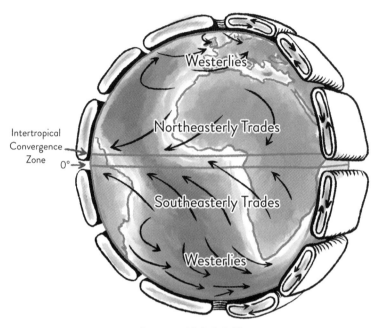

Figure 2: Global Cells

GLOBAL-SCALE WINDS

The equator receives the most direct sunlight on average over the course of a year. Much of the equator is covered by oceans, so lots of heat is stored there. This warm water heats the air above it, causing the air to rise. This is also where the northeast trades and the southeast trades converge, creating a boundary called the intertropical convergence zone (ITCZ). This also helps the air rise. So, along the equator there is the Equatorial Low, a low-pressure system caused by this rising warm air. Along the ITCZ, this rising air creates wet, showery conditions over the equator. This vertical motion of air also means there is very little horizontal surface wind. The region over the equator is sometimes called the doldrums since sailing vessels would often get stuck there as there were no winds to fill their sails.

As this air rises, two things happen. The first, as alluded to in the previous chapter, is the air cools. Think about if you have ever traveled to higher elevation; you usually notice a drop in the temperature. It's roughly 3.5 degrees Fahrenheit for every 1000 feet in the troposphere. This is called the lapse rate, and while it can vary based on the humidity and the stability of the atmosphere, the rule of thumb rate works pretty well.

Eventually, the rising air reaches the tropopause, the boundary layer between the troposphere and the next atmospheric layer, the stratosphere. This layer acts as a barrier that causes the rising air to move laterally. It acts much like a water hose splashing against a window. Some of the air moves north toward the pole, some moves south back toward the equator. The cool air begins to sink down, eventually returning to the surface at about 30 degrees latitude. This convergence area of sinking air creates a high-pressure system, the subtropical high.

This sinking air in these high-pressure systems creates another region where there is very little surface wind. In this area, since the weather is fair, there is no fresh water from rain. This region was called the horse latitudes for a terribly sad reason. When the explorers would hit these areas, they would often throw their horses overboard to conserve drinking water.

When the air reaches the earth's surface, the air again "splashes," with part of it traveling north and south along the earth's surface, where the heating process begins again. This process takes place in both the northern and the southern hemispheres, eventually setting up six large global circulation cells, three north of the equator and three south of the equator. These set up the first piece of the puzzle about the patterns of our weather.

EXERCISE
Wind Knots

Sailors have often used knots to try to affect the winds. In Finland and Lapland mythology, the sea witches were often seen as wind brokers using knotted cord or rawhide strips.[7]

In these stories, the sea witches used pretied knots, then released the winds by untying them. I think you could work in reverse, too, so I will describe making a wind knot cord that would work either way.

You will need
- a length of cord, ribbon, rope, or whatever you would like to use (I use yellow for east/air, but any color you like will do)

Directions
You can do this work anytime. I try to time mine for a nice breezy day when the weather is fair.

Take your cord outside and face the wind. You will be tying a total of three knots. Hold the cord in both hands and visualize the wind spiraling around it, filling it with wind energy.

Once you feel it is saturated with energy, tie the first knot in the center. Say the following as you tie it: "With knot of one, I calm the gale."

Tie a second knot between the middle and the right end of the cord: "With knot of two, wind cease to wail."

Tie the third knot between the middle and the left end of the cord: "With knot of three, just a breeze be."

---

7.   Day, *Quipus and Witches' Knots*, 44–45.

As you visualize the wind calming and being held in the knots, say, "Winds be calmed, so mote it be."

Keep a wind knot cord in your storm protection magic kit. When a storm is headed toward you or your loved ones, use it to do some protection work. Tie it to a tree branch until the storm has passed. I'll give you instructions on making other tools for your storm protection kit in the following chapters.

Reversing the Spell

To reverse, untie the last knot you tied first to raise a breeze: "Let a breeze be."

Then the second knot: "The winds do wail."

Then the first knot (think long and hard about the impact of this! Do you really want to call a gale?): "I call a gale."

I will caution you again about unleashing a gale-force wind. I am sure there are situations where it would be of use, but please be very mindful of safety and impact before you do that work.

CORIOLIS EFFECT

The second piece of the wind pattern puzzle is due to a phenomenon called the Coriolis effect. This effect is caused by the rotation of the earth on its axis. There is a simple thought experiment we can use to understand how the Coriolis effect works.

Imagine you and a friend are standing opposite each other on a playground merry-go-round. The merry-go-round is not moving to start with. Because this is kind of boring, you and your friend decide to play catch by tossing a ball back and forth. As you would expect, the ball travels in a straight line between you and your friend.

Now imagine that the merry-go-round begins to turn counterclockwise, matching the way the earth turns if you were to look down on it from the North Pole. If someone were to watch the game of catch from this vantage point, the ball would still travel in a straight line when you throw it. But, to you and your friend, things have changed. The ball now seems like it is curving off to the right as you throw it back and forth. What is really happening is the ball IS going straight, but you and your friend are moving while it is in flight so that is seems to be traveling a curved path.

This same effect happens to free-moving objects like the ocean currents or wind currents on the earth. In the northern hemisphere, the ocean currents and wind currents seem to deflect to the right. The farther north in latitude we travel, the more pronounced the effect, so the effect is minimal at the equator and strongest at the poles. It is also affected by the speed of the winds—faster winds are deflected more.

For global wind patterns, this means those winds, instead of moving due north or south, are deflected to the right in the northern hemisphere. So, this means we have the northeast trade winds in latitudes from the equator to about 30 degrees, the prevailing westerlies from 30 to 60 degrees, and the polar easterlies above that. Winds are named for the direction they blow from, so the prevailing westerlies are winds that blow from west to east.

EXERCISE
Anemoscopy, Wind Divination

Anemoscopy, with its root *anemos*, the Greek word meaning "wind," is using the wind for divination.

You will need
- an outdoor location
- a way to determine wind direction—a wind vane, a wind sock, or a piece of ribbon

Directions
You can use anemoscopy anytime of day, as long as there is a breeze.

The first way to use this exercise is to stand in your chosen location and observe which way the wind is blowing. Record this direction, then consider what properties you associate with that direction. Sources I use for my personal practice include Dorothy Morrison's *The Craft* and Heron Michelle's *Elemental Witchcraft*. For example, if the wind is from the south, I associate that with the element of fire, the color red, creativity, and fast action.[8]

As you stand in the wind, focus your mind on a situation or project that could benefit from the directional aspect of the wind. In your mind's eye, see the wind take on the color associated with its direction. Let the wind wash over what you see as representing the situation or project, bathing it in that energy. See the color infuse into the object you are visualizing.

The second way you can use this exercise is to have a question in mind or a situation you are seeking guidance for. Follow the steps above and note the wind direction. Use the properties of that direction to provide insight and answers.

For example, you might be having an argument or issue with a friend. You focus on this as you perform your

8. Morrison, *Craft*, 21.

anemoscopy and notice that the wind is blowing from the west, the direction associated with human emotion. The westerly wind is guiding you to act with love and compassion toward your friend, offering them tenderness and forgiveness.[9]

An extension of this form of divination is dust scrying. To do this, simply cast a handful of dust into the wind and take note of the shapes it takes as it settles on the ground. Use these shapes as your divination tool.

EXERCISE
Wind Charging of Magical Tools

An extension of the anemoscopy exercise is to consider what tools of your practice are associated with the wind's direction. Use the wind in the same way you might use sunlight or moonlight for that tool. For example, the tool associated with south/fire is the athame, so a southerly wind could be used to cleanse and charge it.[10]

You will need
- the magical tools you wish to cleanse/charge
- a location where the wind can blow over the tool

Directions
This charging can be done whenever the wind is blowing from the direction you associate with that particular tool. I would caution that you consider what weather might

---

9.   Morrison, *Craft*, 22.

10.   Michelle, *Elemental Witchcraft*, 163.

be coming along with the wind to avoid damaging your tools in a rain- or hailstorm.

Place the tool in a location where the wind can blow across it. Visualize the color you associate with that direction swirling around the tool and being absorbed by it. Once you feel that the tool is sufficiently energized, you are ready to use it again for your practice.

The Coriolis Effect
and Pressure Systems

The Coriolis effect is also the reason why in the northern hemisphere low-pressure systems spin counterclockwise and high-pressure systems spin clockwise. The opposite is true for the southern hemisphere. This applies to highs, lows, and low-pressure storm systems, including hurricanes and typhoons. Small-scale low-pressure systems like tornados generally follow this rule, but on rare occasions, tornados have been known to spin in the opposite direction.

These global circulations give rise to the jet streams. They are strong high-altitude winds that blow west to east and can be thought of as a fast-moving river of air. The jet streams follow boundaries between warm and cold air masses. They can shift north to south seasonally. The jet streams are stronger in the winter because there is a great difference between the temperatures of the warm and cold air.

Even though jet streams are high-atmosphere winds, they do affect conditions closer to the surface. They can create more intense low-pressure systems since, as they blow across the top of the low-pressure system, they draw air out of it, thereby increasing the upward flow of air away from the surface. They can also push high- and low-pressure systems along if they get "caught" in the jet stream's current. However, a weaker, more "buckled" jet stream can trap weather systems in their curves and hold them over an area for a prolonged period.

High-pressure systems are associated with clear skies and fair weather. Here in the Ozarks, in the summer, they can also often be associated with a heat wave; sometimes they are even called heat domes. The high-pressure systems can become so stable they are difficult to dislodge, trapping heat in a region. These can also cause flash droughts in an area. We will return to drought in a later section. Low-pressure systems are generally associated with stormy, rainy, unsettled weather. In fact, the strongest storms, hurricanes, typhoons, and tornados are all forms of low-pressure systems.

EXERCISE
Working with High- or
Low-Pressure Systems

Many traditions consider clockwise as deosil and counter-clockwise as widdershins. Deosil or sunwise is used, for example, to build up magical energy, for manifesting, or for casting a boundary for a ritual space and is the direction high-pressure systems rotate in the northern hemisphere. Deosil can also be associated with good fortune. Widdershins is often the direction used to banish a circle or dispel energy, or sometimes it is associated with bad fortune. It is the direction low-pressure systems rotate in the northern hemisphere.

Think about what you are hoping to achieve with your work. If you are working for calming or stability, choose a high-pressure system. If you are wanting to dispel some energy or break out of a stable but perhaps sti-fling pattern, choose a low-pressure system instead.

You will need

- a weather map or forecast that describes what type of pressure system is local to you
- a piece of paper and writing tool
- a firesafe pan or dish
- matches

Directions

The timing of this working should be when the pressure system is either moving into your area or is already in your area.

To begin this work, write words on the piece of paper that symbolize the situation you are wanting to affect. For example, if I am seeking stability in my workplace, the verse would be something like this:

Stability for me
At work is what I see
My worries now to flee
So mote it be

Next, use a current weather map online or a weather app that shows when the pressure system has moved into your area to know when to begin your working. In my example, I would use the stable weather systems associated with a high-pressure system.

When you are ready to begin, take your writing instrument and begin to circle the words in the same direction as the pressure system—deosil for high pressure, widdershins for low pressure. I would use deosil in my example.

As you make your circles, recite the words you have chosen three times.

Visualize the energy of the pressure system being drawn into the words on the paper.

Once you have completed your work, dispose of the paper by burning it to release your desires into the universe. If you happen to be in a place where this isn't feasible, fold the paper in half instead and tear it into smaller pieces three times, allowing the energy to be set free. Then dispose of it in a waste receptacle and let the magic set in motion do the work.

EXERCISE
Air Flow and Energy Flow Visualization

Another way you can use the energy of these pressure systems is to think about the direction of the airflow that creates the pressure. In a high-pressure system, the air is sinking toward the ground, while in a low, the air is rising in the atmosphere. You can use this airflow to direct energy.

If you are feeling the need to ground yourself, using the downward flow of a high-pressure system would provide an added boost. Likewise, if you are wanting to send out energy, perhaps to a distant friend, low pressure would provide some extra lift. Try this exercise to see how this could work.

You will need

- a quiet location (ideally outside, but anywhere will do)
- a weather map or weather app that shows the movement of the pressure system

Directions to ground

You should time your work for when the pressure system is moving into your area or is present in your area.

First, you will need to ground. Find a quiet place and settle into a comfortable position. Visualize the winds in the upper atmosphere swirling in a deosil manner. Draw this wind and its energy downward, continuing to visualize it spinning. Feel it swirling around you deosil. Feel the energy moving around and through you, ultimately swirling down into the earth.

Once you feel the grounding is complete, release the remainder of the wind and energy to move on its way.

Directions to send energy out

If instead you wanted to send out energy, the process is similar with a few key changes. Visualize the wind at the surface, swirling around you in a widdershins fashion. See the air moving upward, away from the surface. As the air moves upward, see it moving outward toward your intended recipient. Follow the process previously described to end your working.

REGIONAL AND SMALLER-SCALE WIND PATTERNS

There are geographic-scale wind patterns such as the Bermuda high or the Icelandic low that form for similar reasons of heating and cooling. There are also some very interesting regional wind patterns. There isn't as much specific traditional weather lore about these systems, but there are lots of mythologies and legends. Let's look at some of these regional winds.

Katabatic Winds

Katabatic winds are downslope winds that can reach very high speeds, although most do not. Katabatic winds happen when air on plateaus, mountains, or other elevated surfaces cools and becomes denser than the air below it. As it sinks, the air warms and causes winds to move down the slope, and if confined in a narrow canyon, the winds can become quite strong. Some examples of katabatic winds include the piteraq off the icecap in Greenland, the winds off the Antarctic ice sheet, and the williwaw off Tierra del Fuego.

The Santa Anas are a well-known example of a katabatic wind. They originate from the high pressure over the Great Basin of North America as cool, dry winds. Their strength is enhanced by the low-pressure area in the Pacific Ocean off the coast of Southern California. As they descend in elevation, they move through narrow mountain passes that increase their speed. They are also warming up as they descend in elevation.

Because the air was quite dry to begin with, this heating serves to drop the relative humidity of the winds to about 10 percent. By the time the winds reach the coastal areas, they can easily have speeds of forty miles per hour. These winds exacerbate fires during the dry season in Southern California, earning their nickname "devil winds."

Foehn Winds

Another type of downslope wind is the Foehn winds. These are winds that are dry, that warm as they descend, and they can be quite fast. They are formed for a different reason than the Santa Ana–type winds. The Foehn winds are winds that form in the rain shadows of mountain ranges. We will talk more about this in the clouds chapter, but in brief, when winds are forced up over mountains, they lose most of their humidity. As they descend the other side, these dry winds warm up. The Chinook winds that descend the eastern slopes of the Rocky Mountains are a type of Foehn wind. The Chinook winds melt slope snows and cause dramatic temperature changes in their path.

Monsoon Winds

There are other regional winds as well, such as the winds that drive the huge dust storms over the Sahara Desert or created the dust bowl conditions in the Great Plains in the 1930s. One form of these dust storm–causing winds is a haboob. These winds form as a result of the downdrafts along the leading edge of a large thunderstorm and can be dozens of miles wide. They are very common in the Desert Southwest of the United States as well as the African Sudan.

The monsoon winds that bring rainy seasons to parts of the world such as India are seasonally varying winds. A monsoon system is defined as a wind pattern that changes direction seasonally, blowing one direction in the summer and the opposite direction in the winter. In India, the summer monsoon blows northward from the Indian Ocean, carrying humidity and causing a rainy season. In the winter, the direction switches and blows from the north, downslope off the inland plateau, bringing dry conditions to the region. Monsoon conditions occur several places around the world; in the Southwestern United States, the rainy season begins with the midsummer shift of the winds coming from the south-southwest, bringing Pacific moisture to the region.

CRAFT
Ribbon Windsock

Weathervanes aren't just decorative; they give you a sense of the direction the wind is blowing. Because I am obsessed with both weather and vintage farm paraphernalia, I have a small but growing collection of weathervanes. Sometimes I like to take them outside and let them fly free in the wind as they were made to do! Originally, weathervanes were intended to be affixed to the highest point of a barn, house, or other structure. They were designed so that the arrow at the base would swing in the direction the wind was blowing from. I can use my weathervanes as part of my magical practice to work with wind blowing from a particular direction to harness the properties associated with that direction.

Some examples of properties I would associate with the directions:

North: grounding, physical world, day-to-day life issues, hearth and home

East: intellectual pursuits, mental landscape, writing, analytical problems

South: creative energy, passion, spirituality

West: emotions, healing, compassion

A simpler version of this is a windsock. A windsock is a simple tube of lightweight, weather-resistant fabric that can be hung outdoors from a porch, a tree, or another area where it can interact with the wind. They will indicate which direct the wind is blowing and give a general sense of wind speed.

You will need

- a 6-inch plastic embroidery hoop (I recommend plastic since it is more weather resistant)
- a glue gun
- a fray-stopping liquid, either commercial or clear nail polish
- a selection of decorative ribbon cut in two-foot lengths (you can choose all the same type or vary the widths; the design choice is up to you!)

   Note: This is a great project for scrap busting; use up those ribbons you have been saving or the ends of rolls. How much ribbon you need will depend on the width of the ribbons. You will also need four to six extra pieces to cover the outer part of the hoop.
- fishing line and a small swivel eye for hanging

Directions

You can make this craft anytime you wish. It's a great project for kids—exercising caution with the glue gun, of course.

Seal the cut ends of the ribbon with the fray stopper and let dry. Separate the inner and outer parts of the embroidery hoop. Glue one end of the ribbon strips on the *outside part* of the *inner hoop* so that the ribbon ends will be sandwiched between the hoops when you nest them together. Using the extra ribbon strips, wrap the outer hoop to cover it completely. (This is optional; if you like the color of the hoop, you can skip this step. If you do wrap it, make sure the cut ends will be hidden on the inside.)

Tie fishing line to three equidistant points around the outside of the hoop and attach the line to the swivel eye to make the hanger. It is a good idea to secure the fishing line with a drop of glue on the inside of the outer hoop. Nest the inner hoop and outer hoop back together, tightening the outer hoop to secure.

Hang your wind sock and enjoy!

As an extension of this, you could make your ribbon color selection meaningful to your practice; you could put a protection spell on the ribbon or even anoint the hoop with protection oil before assembling your windsock.

Local Wind Patterns

The last type of winds I would like to talk about are the smaller-scale thermal circulations that happen daily, such as land and sea breezes or mountain and valley breezes. Now that you know something about convection, you can probably quickly see how these circulations work. Remember that water and land heat up and cool down at different rates because of their different specific heat capacities.

During the day, the sunlight heats up the land more quickly than the water. The air above the warmer land heats and begins to rise, creating a low-pressure system at the surface. The cooler water creates a surface high-pressure system over it. The pressure imbalance causes a sea breeze, a cool breeze that blows from the sea to the beach. At night, the land cools off more quickly than the water, reversing the conditions so there is a land breeze that blows out toward the sea. These sorts of winds can also occur near large lakes, such as the Great Lakes.

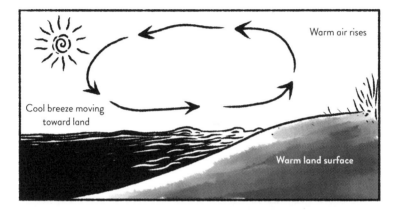

Figure 3: Land and Sea Breezes

In tropical regions, these breezes are year-round occurrences; in the mid-latitudes, they are usually only prevalent in the spring and summer. One example of how they can affect a large area of weather is how they affect the summertime weather patterns in the state of Florida. During the summer, the sea breezes are what cause the predictable afternoon thunderstorms. On the west side, there is a westerly wind from the Gulf of Mexico. These two air masses meeting causes uplift, then add heating convection in the afternoon and you have all the ingredients for afternoon thundershowers.

Another sort of these thermal circulations is the mountain or valley breeze. In the daytime, the valley walls get warmed by the sun, causing the air to heat and begin to rise. This creates a breeze flowing up out of the valley up the mountainside. This valley breeze usually begins in the morning, reaching its peak speed in the afternoon. As the evening approaches, the breeze will wane and eventually it will reverse direction. Now the breeze blows from the mountaintops as the air at higher elevation cools and becomes denser. The mountain breeze will sink down the mountainside and into the valley. These winds are worth paying special attention to if you are hiking or climbing; they can blow up afternoon storms very rapidly on the mountainsides.

One last note: there are many deities associated with winds. I encourage you to research them to see if you find one that resonates with you. I'll talk more about working with winds specific to storms in later chapters.

WEATHER LORE

Much of the weather lore surrounding winds comes from seafaring people. The wind could be both a blessing and a curse to sailors. Not enough wind could mean they were stranded for long periods in one spot in the ocean; too much wind could capsize the vessel. Most of us will never be in a sailing vessel on the ocean, but wind does still impact our daily lives. It can make windchimes sing a pleasant song, or it can cause the garbage can to go on a walkabout down the road! So being able to use weather lore to understand the winds it still a useful tool, even to the non-pirates among us.

> *Red sky at night, sailors' delight …*
> *red sky at morning, sailors take warning.*

Now that you know about the global winds, you can figure out how this phrase is, to some extent, true. First, let's think about how it works in the latitude of the northeast trade winds. The weather patterns there generally follow the northeast trade winds, which means they move east to west. If the red sky at night is caused by the sunset filtering through the clouds, the storm is to the west, which means it has already passed by and we can be delighted about that. The red sunrise could be a result of clouds in the east scattering the sunlight. The clouds in the east means the weather is headed our way, so it will be stormy soon. The red sky is warning us of the approaching storms. Another version of this saying is as follows: "If red the sun begins his race, be sure the rain will fall apace."

These conditions don't work as well in the latitude of the prevailing westerlies. But we can adapt! A red sky at night can also occur when the sun is setting and the sunlight scatters off dust particles in the atmosphere. This can indicate high-pressure and stable air in the west, the direction the weather systems would be coming from. So good weather is on the way. If the high-pressure system is to the east, it could mean there is a low-pressure system moving in from the west to replace it. The warning of the eastern sky is that the low-pressure system is coming and stormy weather could be on the way.

> *When the wind is from the east,*
> *it's neither good for man nor beast.*

Again, this saying originates from latitudes where the weather systems are influenced by the prevailing westerlies. So, weather patterns tend to move west to east. If a system is coming from the east, that usually means it is associated with a low-pressure system circulating counterclockwise. Remember, the weather associated with a low is usually unsettled and stormy.

> *The stars twinkle, we cry WIND.*

This Maltese saying is mostly true. Stars are point sources of light unlike the light from the planets, so the light we see from them can be affected by the turbulence of the atmosphere. If there are strong winds, the atmosphere will be turbulent, so the stars will clearly twinkle.

> *Whistling up a storm.*

This phrase comes from the lore that aboard a boat, whistling was forbidden for fear it would bring bad weather. The idea was that whistling was a challenge to the winds, causing them to rise and bring a storm. Sometimes, though, sailors might have whistled on purpose if they were stuck in a windless area in hopes of getting a jumpstart to their progress.

When the ditch and pond offend the nose,
look for rain and stormy blows.

This saying describes the effect of a low-pressure system moving into an area. A high-pressure system normally keeps the earthy scented molecules contained near their source. If a low-pressure system moves in, it allows the molecules to spread out, and so we smell the ditch and pond! Low-pressure systems often bring rainy or stormy weather, so the odor is a clue that rainy weather is on the way.

No weather's ill if the winds be still.

Calm conditions are usually associated with high-pressure systems, so this saying is generally considered true. Strong winds are usually associated with frontal boundaries where the weather is likely to be changing soon. There are some cases where this is patently untrue, such as the "calm before the storm" of an approaching storm creating an updraft that is causing the wind to change directly and temporarily appear calm. "The eye of the storm," such as a hurricane eye, can often be a region of high pressure with clear skies and calm winds. This is obviously a temporary situation before the remainder of the hurricane passes through.

The winds of daytime wrestle and fight
longer and stronger than those of the night.

This saying can generally be seen as true since the daytime heating of the sun causes the air to heat and be more unstable. Unstable air generates winds that can be turbulent and strong at times. At night, cooler temperatures lend stability to the air and the winds die down. There are cases where this doesn't hold true, however. If a frontal system moves into the area, the winds can be strong regardless of if it is daytime or nighttime. As you will find with most weather lore, even for the ones that are pretty well accepted as accurate, there are always conditions that make them inaccurate!

> *When the glass falls low, prepare for a blow.*
> *When the glass rides high, let your kites fly.*

I chose this one because of how I dearly love flying a kite! Some of my fondest memories of my mom include us getting new kites every spring and flying them. The "glass" refers to a type of barometer. A weatherglass was generally a water-filled open-type barometer that would look somewhat like a teapot. There would be a reservoir of water and a long slender spout or neck that was open at the end to the atmosphere.

When the air pressure was low, water would rise into the neck, causing the level in the reservoir to drop. Alternately, when the pressure was high, the water was pushed down and out of the spout, causing the level in the reservoir to rise. Low pressure could mean storms are on the way, so prepare for them. High pressure brings good weather, but sadly sometimes this means little surface wind. Hopefully there will be enough of a breeze to let the kites fly!

> *When down the chimney falls the soot,*
> *mud will soon be underfoot.*

This is another version of the same phrase. Again, the instability keeps the smoke from rising, and the soot it carries will not be blown away. The corollary to this, "When the smoke rises high, good weather is nigh," is because the stable atmosphere allows the warm air of the smoke to rise.

WINDING IT UP

These large-scale wind patterns are the foundation of all other weather systems. They affect every part of the planet and touch every life in some way. The smaller regional winds may not affect my life directly, but they can have a ripple effect on the weather in my area. Wind has a long reach.

This isn't unlike magic. Magical work for healing, protection, good fortune, and so on can have just as far-reaching impact. How many times have you done healing work for a friend on the other side of the country or the world? Wind seems to be the perfect choice for a magical ally to help boost magic. Winds are a global phenomenon, and maybe if we consider them as far-reaching sources of energy, we can make use of their energy in that way. Even just considering the simple idea of the direction of their motion can add to our energy work tool kit.

I hope you take the time to get to know about your local wind patterns and then see where you can incorporate some of these ideas into your magical practice.

Chapter 3
THE MAGIC AND ENERGY OF OCEAN CURRENTS

The ocean is a huge source of energy for storm systems, winds, and other weather phenomena. The water, because of its high specific heat capacity, stores heat from the sun very effectively. Because much of the surface of the earth is covered with water, understanding how it contributes to our weather is important.

The ocean water absorbs most of the sunlight that makes it to the earth's surface. Not only do the oceans store this heat, but they also help distribute it. One way this happens is through evaporation of water from the oceans' surfaces. The evaporation of water from the ocean increases the humidity and temperature of the air above it.

HUMIDITY

Since I've mentioned it several times, now is a good time to talk about the definition of humidity. Most anyone who lives in the Southern United States can describe how humid air feels, but let's dig into the scientific description. Humidity is broadly defined as the concentration of water vapor in the atmosphere.

Relative humidity is usually expressed as a percentage. It is the ratio of the amount of humidity currently present in the air to the maximum amount of humidity the air can hold based on its temperature. The higher the percentage, the more humid or "muggy" the air is. Depending on temperature, air can hold different amounts of water before it becomes saturated. Warm air can hold more water vapor than an equivalent amount of cold air.

Humid air can prevent people and animals from cooling themselves off by sweating or panting since evaporation is limited by the moisture already present in the air. This causes the dangerous conditions that lead to heat exhaustion or heat stroke. The heat index was developed by combining the air temperature in the shade and the relative humidity to give an effective or "feels like" temperature.

The dewpoint is the temperature at which a parcel of air is considered saturated and water vapor will condense out of the air to form dew. Usually this happens when warm, humid air cools overnight, reaching its dewpoint. At this point, the relative humidity would be 100 percent.

Most precipitation on Earth starts this part of its journey being evaporated from the oceans. It enters the air as water vapor and journeys long thanks to the winds. The oceans have a huge impact on our weather, even for those of us who are landlocked.

CURRENTS

The ocean currents are created by several factors. Surface currents are due to the wind blowing water along the surface, the rotation of the earth causing the Coriolis effect, and whatever landforms the water encounters on its journey. As the surface water is pushed along, water from below the surface of the ocean upwells to fill the space. These upwelling currents are important to coastal areas as they bring nutrients to the surface and help the marine life population. Other factors that create ocean currents are density variations due to temperature or salinity differences, underwater geological activity, and underwater terrain changes.

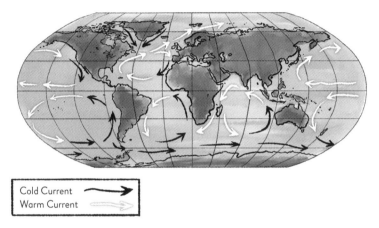

Cold Current
Warm Current

Figure 4: Ocean Currents

The currents created by the temperature and salinity difference are called the thermohaline circulation or, more grandly, the global conveyor belt. These currents circulate around the entire globe. The starting point for these currents is considered to be in the North Atlantic near the North Pole. Water here is cold and has a higher saline concentration due to the sea ice freezing with a lower salt concentration and leaving behind the extra salt. The cold water is dense, so it sinks toward the ocean floor, causing surface water to flow to the area to replace it.

The deepwater current heads southward across the globe, where it warms and rises. The current continues to move south, eventually arriving at Antarctica. The current skirts the edge of the continent, getting colder and sinking deeper. This has the effect of reenergizing the current as it continues its journey. Eventually it splits into two northward-moving currents, one in the Indian Ocean, the other in the Pacific. As these two branches heading north warm and rise again, they create areas of upwelling. These two currents loop southward and eventually return to the South Atlantic, moving northward where they complete their journey. The current moves quite slowly, and some estimate that it can take a given parcel of water about a thousand years to complete the entire circuit.

Gulf Stream

Another important part of this conveyer system is the Gulf Stream and its northern extension, the North Atlantic Drift. It comes from the Atlantic North Equatorial Current, which is a result of the northeast trade winds, and moves west from Africa. The Gulf Stream is a warm, fast-moving ocean current that originates off the tip of Florida and travels up the east coast of North America. As it moves off the end of Newfoundland, it crosses the Atlantic toward Europe. The Gulf Stream affects the climate and weather of North America's East Coast and Western Europe.

Ocean currents are another formidable source of energy for magical working. There are many deities associated with the oceans you could work with (going into all of them is way beyond this book's scope). There are also many myths about the ocean and its power, so learning more about these would enhance your practice. For now, I'll focus on how to incorporate the energy of these ocean currents into magical practice.

EXERCISE
Ocean Currents Meditation

Watching an animated map of ocean currents can be very calming. Look online for one. I try to find a map that shows the ocean currents with the ocean temperatures as an overlay. Using those together makes it easy to see how the energy is moving around the earth. If you don't have access to an animated map, a static map will also work just as well. You could even print out a global map and draw the ocean currents yourself if you can't find one you like.

You will need
- a quiet space
- an animated map of the ocean currents
- calming music (optional)
- other items that make your meditations more effective (optional)

Directions
Time this work whenever you need a few minutes to find calmness or peace during your day. I especially like to use it during my lunch break on challenging days at work.

Find a quiet place where you can be free from distraction during your meditation. If desired, play some music that helps you relax.

Open up the map, setting up for a full-scale global view so you can visualize the ocean current conveyor belt as it circles the globe. Before beginning to follow the currents, take a moment to close your eyes and take some deep, cleansing breaths. Try to make the exhale last longer than the inhale on each breath. I recommended at least three cleansing breaths before proceeding.

Open your eyes and settle on a starting point on the map. Focusing only on the motion of the currents, allow your eyes to follow the path they take. If you find yourself getting distracted, simply refocus on the last point you remember seeing on the map and begin again.

As you follow the path of the currents around the map, imagine the waters warming and cooling as they move along their journey. Feel the energy of the ocean current flowing through you, calming you and bolstering your sense of peace.

Take this journey along the currents at your own pace; there isn't a one-size-fits-all speed here. Allow your eyes to drift along the map without forcing them to follow the currents at a certain speed.

Once you have returned to your starting point, do a quick check-in with yourself. How do you feel? Are you feeling calmer? Have your heart rate and breathing rate slowed? Do you feel refreshed? If not, feel free to follow the path again, time permitting. This is your practice, so you can take the time you need.

If you feel ready after your check-in, close your eyes once more, allowing your body and mind to absorb the calm energy you gathered up during your meditation.

Take a deep breath in, and on the exhale, thank the ocean and other spirits or energies you wish to acknowledge.

Exercise extension

An extension of this activity is to journal about any thoughts or feelings you experienced during your meditation. Describe any images that popped up during the activity. You might also pay attention to places your eyes wanted to linger. Is there some significance to those places? Spend time researching them and make note of anything that resonates with you.

Ocean Gyres

The larger currents create boundaries for small areas of circulation called ocean gyres. These large areas of ocean current circulation are due to the impact of the Coriolis effect on the ocean currents. The gyres are responsible for the formation of "seas" in the oceans, such as the Sargasso Sea in the Atlantic, oceanic "deserts" where there is a lack of biologic activity, and the location of the oceanic garbage patches full of microplastics and other pollution. There are five major ocean gyres: the North and South Atlantic, the North and South Pacific, and the Indian Ocean gyres. There is some evidence that because these gyres redistribute heat, they may serve as mechanisms that weaken tropical cyclones such as typhoons and hurricanes.

The transport of energy by the ocean conveyer belts helps moderate the temperatures on the planet. These belts transport heat away from the equator, which keeps the temperatures from being too extreme. The heat that is transported to the poles keeps them from becomes too frigid. Because the earth's surface is always going to be unevenly heated, there will always be both wind and ocean currents.

El Niño and La Niña

Just like no magic exists in a bubble, the effect of the oceans thousands of miles away from my home has an impact on the weather here in the Ozarks. Earth's oceans are huge heat sinks, since water is so effective at storing the thermal energy from the sun. So, even though I live far from the ocean, it still affects the weather where I live.

A perfect example of this is the El Niño or La Niña effect. This is a phenomenon that happens in the tropical Eastern Pacific, just off the coast of South America. The normal or "neutral" conditions that happen over the tropical Pacific are caused by the northeast trade winds. The winds push the warm surface water westward across the Pacific until it essentially "piles up" off the east side of Australia and Indonesia. This warm air as you now might expect will create unstable rainy conditions there.

Back to the east, cooler water from deeper in the Pacific rises up, or upwells, off the western side of South America. This cool water causes the weather patterns near the coast to be very stable—not much stormy weather, or in some areas even rain is a rarity.

El Niño and La Niña happen when there is a change in the strength of the northeast trades. There is a trade-off of warm and cold currents in an irregular pattern that occurs every few years. This is the Southern Oscillation and is responsible for creating the conditions for either an El Niño or a La Niña effect.

El Niño frequently happens around the Christmas period. Weaker-than-normal winds mean less warm water is pushed away from South America. The surface of the Eastern Pacific near the equator becomes warmer than average. This causes downwelling of warmer water in the east and upwelling of colder water in the west. The weather off western South America becomes more unsettled and rainier, which in turn causes the weather in the Western Pacific to become dryer and more stable. El Niño events can last several months and sometimes even over a year.

After an El Niño event, the trade winds can go back to their normal pattern and strength. However, sometimes they can rebound and become stronger than normal. This causes the reverse effect of an El Niño. The Eastern and Central Pacific become colder than normal. This creates very stable air over the Eastern Pacific with rainier, unsettled conditions over the Western Pacific. This is a La Niña condition. La Niña events can last longer than El Niño events, sometimes even two or three years.

Clearly these events will impact the regions where they occur, such as Peru and Ecuador. You may wonder why I am interested in events that occur in the Pacific Ocean when I live in the Arkansas Ozarks. These events, as it turns out, have strong influences on the weather in North America, so they impact me and my farm directly. El Niño causes the Pacific jet stream to move farther south, so it causes there to be warmer-than-normal conditions in the Northern Plains and Pacific Northwest. There will be wetter conditions over the Southwest. In my part of the country, it can lead to colder-than-normal winters and wetter conditions overall. While that might not sound bad, even with rain, too much of a good thing is still too much.

La Niña pushes the Pacific jet farther north than normal. The effect in the Lower 48 is essentially the opposite of what El Niño does. The Northern Plains are colder overall, and the Pacific Northwest is wetter. The Upper Mississippi and Ohio Valley regions are warmer and wetter than normal. In my area, it is warmer but drier. La Niña conditions can turn into drought conditions, and a strong flash drought can wreak havoc on the agricultural community in my area.

ACTIVITY
Building an Ocean Energy Altar

Even though the ocean may be far from where you live, the energy moved by the ocean currents certainly impacts the weather all over the world. Collecting things that represent the ocean and the energy it moves around the earth is a good way to remind you that you can tap into this energy even if you live in a landbound area.

You will need
- a space to build your altar
- a statue of an ocean deity should you choose to work with one
- items that represent the ocean and the energy it moves, such as ocean water, sea glass, beach sand, a map of ocean currents, and seashells

    Note: Sea glass is a great representation of the power the ocean has to shape and soften things over time. Seashells that have washed ashore can represent the motion of the tides and the energy of this cycling ebbing and flowing.

Directions
Gather your items. Some of these items may only be accessible if you purchase them, which is just fine. Remember to source your shells from ethical traders when possible. If I have a friend taking a trip to the ocean, they know to expect a text asking them to pick up bits and bobs for me.

Collecting ocean water is a good way to harness the energy there. Collect it on a calm, clear day for protective or calming work or on a windy, active day for energizing a situation. Always leave an offering behind to thank the ocean deities for allowing you to take some of the water. If you aren't able to get to the ocean directly, you could sketch the ocean waves or find a photo to use instead. The same ideas apply to collecting beach sand.

Once you have assembled your items, build your altar in a style that suits your practice.

ACTIVITY AND EXERCISE
Creating and Using Ocean Energy Healing Bowl

Once you have created an ocean energy altar, it is the perfect place to do healing work.

You will need
- a bowl of your preferred style that is large enough to hold your items
- cleansing method (incense, sea salt, rattles, etc.)
- ocean water
- beach sand
- sea glass or seashells to represent those who need healing energy
- other ocean-related items, such as coral and sand dollars (optional)

Directions

The timing of creating the bowl is whenever it is needed, but if it isn't an emergency situation, you could choose the timing to match a day of the week or a moon phase that would most benefit the healing process.[11]

If you are working with any ocean deities, you may invite them to attend your working.

Cleanse your items using your preferred method. I use dried basil and sage from my own garden. You could also wash everything in sea salt and warm water if it is safe to do so.

Place the bowl on your ocean energy altar. Place a layer of beach sand at the bottom of the bowl. Place your sea glass or seashells to represent the person or people you are creating the bowl for. If you wish, you could add food coloring to the water to represent the healing energy.

Slowly pour the ocean water into the bowl so as to keep the disturbance of the sand to a minimum. Once the sand has settled, begin your healing work.

Visualize the energy contained in the sand and water infusing the shells or glass. If you want to speak a verse you have created or one you have found, do that three times as you continue your visualization. Take as long as you need in this visualization.

Once you are satisfied with the energy you have infused your pieces with, leave them in the bowl to continue to draw from the healing energies of the water and sand. Thank any ocean deities you may have worked with for their help.

---

11. Weston, *Ozark Mountain Spell Book*, 16–19.

Exercise extension

Old sailor folklore says that pouring oil on the seas has a calming effect.[12] If you feel that the health situation is a particularly challenging one for the person and they would benefit from some extra calming energy, try using some magically charged oil or even just plain olive oil. Put a few drops of it on the surface of the water in your healing bowl as you focus on the extra calming energy going to the person you are doing the healing work for.

If you don't have access to ocean water, regular water will do. If you look at the water cycle, all the water on the planet spent time in the ocean at some point.[13] Using the water you have available is always better than using none at all, in my opinion.

WEATHER LORE

There isn't any lore that specifically addresses the ocean currents, but there is some lore that is tied to weather on specific days that might be related to El Niño and La Niña.

If it rains much during the twelve days after Christmas,
it will be a wet year.

In my area, El Niño brings wetter-than-normal winters but also heats the part of the Pacific Ocean that affects the weather in the southern United States. The warmer ocean temperatures lead to more instability and a wetter long-term forecast.

---

12. Behroozi, "The Calming Effect of Oil on Water," 407–414.

13. Britannica, "Water Cycle."

When it is hottest in June, it will be coldest
in the corresponding days of the next February.

La Niña creates hotter, dryer conditions where I live but that means the winter will be colder than normal as well. So this phrase could hold true if La Niña conditions persist through the winter into the early spring.

Heavy September rains bring drought.

These two weather patterns can also be attributed to extremes in weather. Unusually heavy rains in an area over a prolonged period or a drought are both caused by El Niño and La Niña events depending on what part of the continent you are on.

If the first week in August is unusually warm,
the winter will be white and long.

There is not really any direct connection to those patterns, but it seems like they speak to long-term patterns that could be caused by El Niño or La Niña. The weather on the Omen Days, December 26 through January 6, for example, is supposed to be a weather predictor for the corresponding month of the year. This could also be extended to things like Groundhog Day lore or the Ember Days.

If the first of July be rainy weather,
it will rain more or less for three weeks together.

This is a saying my grandpa often shared and is a version of the previous one. He would say that if it rained July 1, it would rain for fifteen days straight. Being an early July Cancer who did *not* want rain on my birthday, I didn't approve of this message! Granted, it wasn't constant rain but usually those typical summertime weather patterns of thunderstorms in the afternoon. That meant it needed that warm Gulf air fed by the evaporation of warm water in the Gulf current loops.

Winding It Up

The ocean and its currents may seem far removed from my Ozark farm, but it still has a tremendous impact on the weather I experience. The weather patterns across all of North America are driven by the ocean currents and the energy they carry. Using my scientific knowledge to understand their influence helps me be better prepared on my farm in case of drought or too much rain.

From a magical perspective, the oceans are huge energy banks. Thinking about how the ocean currents rise and fall as they move on their journey could be useful when thinking about timing on a magical working that is meant to ebb and flow. Or imagine them circling the earth, building the energy and moving it from place to place. There are many ways you could incorporate ocean currents into an energy work practice. I encourage you to let your mind set sail on the ocean blue and see where it takes you in your magical practice.

Chapter 4
FRONTAL SYSTEMS
Magic Sweeping Down the Plains

The type of weather that is literally on the horizon is determined by the type of frontal boundary that is moving in. We have all noticed the effect of these even if we aren't actively looking at the weather. Have you ever gone to work dressed for warm weather and come out desperately wishing you had your winter coat? Maybe you have been the unfortunate victim of day after day of rain causing flooding. For those of us who live in Tornado Alley, we know that a cold front blowing in after several days of hot, humid weather may well mean a long night of being in our hidey-hole with kids, pets, and the weather radio.

In my magical practice, these fronts carry waves of energy that are available for my spell work. I can look at their temperatures, their speed, the type of weather they produce, or even the clouds they form and fold that into my energy work. The frontal system is the foundation of all those other energies, so understanding how they work and what they carry with them makes my magical work more powerful. By keeping my eyes to the sky, I can use the signs nature gives us to predict what is likely coming in the next few hours or days. Forewarned is forearmed, so I can make the preparations I need in both my magical life and my mundane daily life.

AIR MASSES

What is a front? It is a boundary separating air masses with different characteristics. These characteristics include temperature, humidity, and wind. These differences often cause instability in the atmosphere, which then generates weather.

Let's start by defining what an air mass is. Parcels of air are defined by their humidity and temperature. The most widely used classification system is the Bergeron process. It uses a system of letters to describe the air.

The first letter describes the moisture level, or humidity. Continental (c) is air that originates over land, so is generally dry air. Maritime (m), as you might guess, originates over water, so is humid air. The next letter describes the source region of the air, which gives an idea about its temperature. Tropical (T) comes from warmer regions, Polar (P) comes from colder regions, and Arctic or Antarctic (A) comes from very cold regions. There are other classifications in both these categories, but to keep from sounding too much like a meteorology text, I will focus on these.

Air that sweeps into the Ozarks from central Canada would be continental Polar (cP). It is cool or cold air that is dry and fast moving. In contrast, air that comes up from the south from the Gulf of Mexico is maritime Tropical (mT). This is that warm humidity that causes us to say, "It's not the heat, it's the humidity!" This warm, humid air is generally slower moving than the dry air because it is heavier from the water vapor.

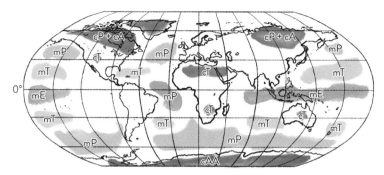

Figure 5: Air Masses

ACTIVITY
Weather-Related Health and the Stones That Are Allies

Often people find themselves affected physically in some way by these different air mass, pressure, and frontal systems. Some people have headaches or joint aches ahead of a cold front leading a low-pressure system. Other people find that the heavy moist air of a warm front or the stagnant effects of a high-pressure system might affect breathing. I find I may feel nervous or anxious during a time with the atmosphere is unsettled and the winds are shifting, such as when a frontal system is approaching. I like wearing different types of stones or crystals during these times that give some relief.

You will need
- a book on stone properties
- a weather app or weather forecast

- a bowl of seawater for cleansing
- stones appropriate to weather-induced health issues (for example, hematite for relief from headaches and joint pain tied to changes in pressure,[14] larimar for relief from sinus pain due to weather changes, and malachite for joint pain[15])

Directions

Timing for this working ideally would be in advance of the weather that causes the health issue. You can use these stones just as they are, or you could create a jewelry piece out of them.

Cleanse your stones in a seawater bath if it is safe to do so for the stone or jewelry. If desired, sit the stones out in the sunlight or in the full moon to allow them to gather the solar or lunar energies for added benefit.

Carry your stones or wear the jewelry during the weather event. When the weather has passed, cleanse the jewelry again and store for the next weather-related health issue.

Exercise extension

Use your ocean energy healing bowl from the previous chapter to suffuse more healing energy into your stones.

WEATHER FRONTS

Fronts form where different air masses meet up. The type of front is determined by which air mass is moving into the area. You have likely seen weather maps on TV with the symbols of the fronts. Those symbols describe the "vital statistics" of the front, and with

---

14. Palmer, *Healing Power of Crystals*, 198.

15. Simmons and Ahsian, *Book of Stones*, 277.

a little practice, the weather can be predicted reasonably accurately just by looking at the maps.

Warm Fronts

I'll start with warm fronts. Warm air will advance into an area where colder air is receding. The warm air is less dense than the cold air, so the two air parcels will not mix. Even though the warm is advancing on the cold air, the boundary between the two forms gradually, without a steep slope. This gradual overtaking of the warm air by the cold forces the warm air up.

As the air rises, it cools, and any moisture it might be carrying condenses to form clouds. In a later chapter, I will talk more about the types of clouds that form and how to use these as predictors of weather to come. For now, I will just describe the weather that happens. When the warm front arrives, it is accompanied by steady rain or snow showers that can sometimes have quite heavy precipitation. Also, the temperature will increase with the front's passage. Severe storms are not usually associated with a warm front.

Cold Fronts

Contrast this situation with a cold front. A cold front will form where cold air moves rapidly into an area that warm air is occupying. The cold air is denser and faster moving, so it wedges underneath the warm, humid air. It forces it up rapidly, creating a much steeper frontal boundary than a warm front. The steep boundary means the phase change of vapor condensing to liquid then eventually freezing to ice happens quickly and in a limited area, so the storms associated with the cold front tend to be much stronger and often can be severe. I will delve into storms in a later chapter since they are an awe-inspiring energetic phenomenon.

Other Fronts

Occluded fronts happen when a cold front overtakes a warm front. The word *occlusion* means "closed off," and that is essentially what a cold front does in the atmosphere. It forces the warm moist air aloft, holding it suspended until the water vapor has condensed and forms rain or snow. These fronts are the ones that often bring extended periods of heavy rain or snow.

A stationary front is, as its name implies, a frontal boundary with little or no movement. The winds blow parallel to this frontal boundary, keeping it from advancing. The weather associated with the stationary front is usually partly cloudy with perhaps some light precipitation.

Fronts on Weather Maps

Looking at a weather map to learn to identify these fronts is another tool in the tool kit for magical and energy working. The symbols for the fronts give a clue about their temperature, their speed, and the direction they are moving. A warm front is symbolized by red half circles; a cold front is represented by blue triangles. The occluded front is purple with the combination of cold and warm front symbols facing the direction the front is traveling. The symbol for a stationary front is also a combination of cold and warm front symbols, but they are facing opposite directions to indicate the front isn't moving. The triangles are meant to show the motion of the cold front is "sharp" and rapid as it passes through. The warm front uses half circles to be a reminder that its motion is more gradual than that of the cold front.

EXERCISE
Magical Fronts

Make yourself a chart for each front type, then add what you know about the temperature change, the weather associated with it, the speed it moves at, and so on.

You will need
- paper
- a ruler
- writing instruments of multiple colors to correspond to temperatures of the front

Directions
Make this chart whenever you are ready to start exploring the energy of fronts.

Type of Front	Temp.	Clouds	Winds	Precipitation	Magical Correspondences
Cold					
Warm					
Occluded					
Stationary					

Turn the paper so your table is in landscape orientation. Make five rows (one for labels, four for types of fronts). The top row will be your labeling row. The other rows will be labeled as follows: cold, warm, occluded, stationary.

Make at least six columns: type of front, temperature, clouds, winds, precipitation, magical correspondences.

Using the scientific knowledge from this chapter, fill out the first four columns.

Take some time to list all the magical correspondences and connections you can think of for each front. You may find it helpful to add more columns to organize your ideas. This is a great time to dig into your library or do some online research from trusted sources. Honestly, one of the most powerful tools is your own intuition, so if you need someone to give you permission to trust your intuition, I am here for it!

Once you have finished your chart, you now have a handy quick-reference guide to plan your magical work!

Exercise extension

Draw a current weather map or a desired future weather map as you are preparing to do energy work so you can get a big-picture view of what is happening with the weather. You can easily find a blank map template. You could choose to focus on just your area or be more expansive by looking at the country or even the continent. Print out a blank map, then fill it in with colored pencils or pens. For example, I will print out a map of North America, and then go online to the National Weather Service to their Graphical Forecast section. This is a data junkie's dream. The map I look at first is the current daily forecast map, which has all the currently active fronts and pressure systems. Once you have a current map, you can see clearly what timing you should use for your magical practice.

I know this sounds a little bit like I am asking you to do homework for science class. But I think my energy work is most effective when I'm using my map and reference table as a guide, looking for weather that supports the work I am trying to do. I will draw the fronts on the map; I may even try to draw in symbols for the weather I want, write my intention, color, sketch, or whatever I feel I need to do to put the work into motion. I find this tool especially effective if I want to perhaps send energy to a friend in another part of the country, if I or my beloved ones are traveling and need fair weather, or if I have an outdoor event coming up. I draw the map with the desired conditions to achieve my end goal.

WEATHER LORE

Since weather fronts bring with them specific types of weather, it certainly pays to be able to predict what's coming! For centuries, farmers have been the best observational meteorologists, and then science was able to use the observations and discovery to improve accuracy and timing of forecasts. Obviously now we are surrounded by technology that makes this easier. However, as a witch, there is powerful energy in being able to connect with nature and weather directly.

The sharper the blast,
the sooner 'tis past.

The cold fronts are moving in rapidly with a sharper temperature change and often stormy weather, but the storms move through quickly. You may have experienced a day where you went into an event and the weather was warm, maybe a little humid. A couple or three hours later when the event was over, you came out to stormy cold rain or maybe even sleet or snow. The cold front that blew through while you were enjoying the event is the reason!

The first and last cold fronts are the worst.

This again works in my latitude to a degree. It is rooted in agricultural history. The last cold front of spring and the first cold front of fall often herald the dates of the last freeze of spring and the first freeze of fall. Cold fronts, remember, clear out the air, making the nights clear, which means the temperatures could dip below freezing during these times. Any crops planted early or still in the fields to be harvested could be at risk. I know I have run outside many times with every spare bowl, cooking pot, towel, and sheet to protect my plants from damage.

Rain before seven,
fine before eleven.

This saying can be true if the rain is caused by a cold front. Cold fronts move quickly and will clear an area within a few hours. However, a warm front will move slower and may take longer to clear out an area. A stationary front may hover over an area for a couple of days or maybe longer.

When the icy wind warms,
expect snowstorms.

This saying can be true. It is referring to a warm front passing through an area in the winter. Warm fronts carry more moisture than the cold air, so if they enter an area, the temperatures will rise. If they do stay below freezing, the precipitation will be frozen and it may possibly snow. As it turns out, it takes specific conditions for snow to form. Not to worry, we will look in detail at winter precipitation in its own chapter.

The west wind always brings wet weather.
The east wind, wet and cold together.
The south wind surely brings the rain.
The north wind blows it back again.

This saying, at least at my latitude, is partially true. Cold fronts often approach from the north or northwest. The leading edge of the front pushed along by the westerlies will often bring rain. Then the skies clear as the cold front "blows it back again," pushing rain out of the area. Southerly flow winds bring humidity into my area, which also can cause rain when met with the cold front. Easterly winds very often are due to a low-pressure system, which will push a series of fronts through an area and bring their associated weather along for the ride.

Rain foretold, long last. Short notice, soon will pass.

Often, systems that produce major rain or snow events are associated with slower-moving occluded or warm fronts. Their arrival is heralded a day or two ahead of time often by the cloud forms. We will talk more about this in the chapter about clouds. Storms, however, can crop up in a matter of a few hours from a cold front. So there is much less advance notice of those systems.

When the night has a fever,
it cries in the morning.

If the temperatures rise at night, that means a warm front has moved into the area. The warm front will most likely bring rain along with it, so it could very well rain in the morning.

WINDING IT UP

So how can we use these ideas for our energy and magical work? One way I begin is I write down everything I know about the physics of the particular frontal system. For a cold front, for example, I would write down temperature drop, fast movement, and stormy weather. I would do the same for the warm front and occluded front. Next, I write down what kind of work I am needing and wanting to do. Let's say I want to cool off a situation. In that case, using the dropping temperature of a cold front would be a good choice. What about if I want to nurture a new idea, situation, or relationship? Maybe the gentle rains or snow of a warm front would be a better choice. For deep cleansing, maybe the extended rains or snows that come from an occluded front would be my choice.

A useful tool I have is a simple weather station. You can find these in a variety of retailers and spend as much money as you care to on them. For my purposes, I choose a less expensive one for use at my farm. I also equip myself with other trusted weather sources through our local office of the National Weather Service. The science gives me enough lead time on conditions that I am able to make whatever preparations I need both physically on my farm and in my magical practice.

Now that you have a better understanding of how these frontal systems move energy from place to place on our planet, can you imagine ways that you might use them in your practice? Start with something small, maybe journaling how you feel as a certain weather pattern approaches. Make a planner that lets you prepare for the next front so you can have your tools ready to absorb some of the energy from it. Using weather maps is a great way to start that planning! Once you understand the energy the fronts move, all of that is at your disposal for working.

·

Chapter 5

CLOUDS

Portals for Imagination and Magic

When was the last time you just lay back in the shade of a friendly tree and looked at the clouds? Often as children, we would use the clouds as portals for our imagination. Clouds were the gateway to magic and wonderment for many of us. They still should be.

Clouds are storehouses of energy to tap into for magical work. The rich processes that build a cumulonimbus, for example, contain all the energy of the oceans, of the winds, of the sun, and of the water phases. Everything that goes into making this cloud adds to its energy bank. If I draw on that energy for my magical work, I have it all at my disposal.

The clouds are still there, waiting for us to rediscover them with new eyes. Go outside and rediscover that magic!

CLOUD TYPES

What is a cloud? Scientifically speaking, it is a collection of ice and liquid water particles; some clouds contain only one form, while others are a mixture of the two. It is the physical manifestation

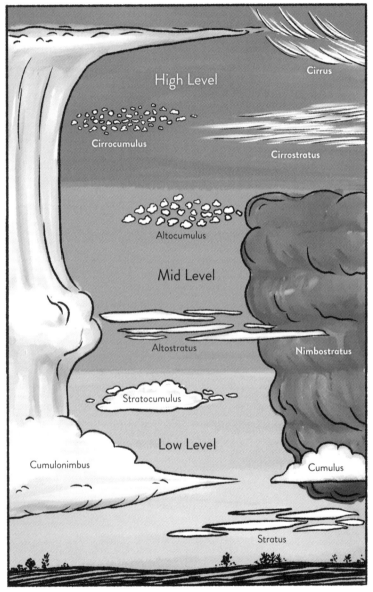

Figure 6: Cloud Types

of the energy release of phase changes. As you look at the cloud, you can see the process of energy building upward and reaching a peak as the cloud is formed by the water vapor first becoming liquid water then possibly freezing into ice.

Understanding Latin name origins gives me the ability to describe quickly what the cloud looks like. Some of the names tell me about where the cloud is in the atmosphere, some tell a little bit about their shape, while others describe what kind of precipitation is coming from them. Knowing these descriptions can also tell me about what the cloud is made of and even why it formed. I'm an information fan—the more I can know about something, the better!

Let's start with the names that tell you about where the clouds form in the atmosphere.

High Clouds

Cirrus-/Cirro-prefixed clouds form the highest in the troposphere. They are thin, wispy, and icy. *Cirrus* (Ci) means "lock of hair," so cirrus clouds often remind me of the bits of hair left behind after getting a haircut. They are sometimes called mare's tails because of their wispy appearance. Cirrus clouds are some of the first clouds to appear for all types of weather fronts. Cirrus clouds tell me some kind of precipitation is on the way! My papaw often called them snow clouds since they were easier to see in the winter due to the sun's lower angle.

Cirrostratus (Cs) clouds are high (cirro) and layered (stratus). Usually, they are so thin and icy they can't be seen during the day. It will look like any other clear day, but at night, these thin layers can catch the moonlight and reflect it, creating the ring around the moon. Cirrostratus clouds are one of the leading clouds of a warm front that can bring rain or snow. So "ring around the moon, rain or snow by noon" means the cirrostratus clouds are here and soon the warm front will bring its weather too.

Cirrocumulus clouds are the rarest of these three kinds to form. They look like very high, small cotton balls in the sky. *Cumulus* means "piles" or "heaps," like the familiar cumulus humilis or fair-weather cumulus clouds seen on a bright sunny day. Cirrocumulus clouds have a similar shape but are much smaller than their cloud cousins. They form when turbulence interacts with an existing cirrus layer, causing them to form as short-lived transitional clouds.

Midlevel Clouds

Middle-level clouds have the prefix *alto-* in their names. There are two main types of midlevel clouds. They also have their own weather lore sayings that go along with them. Alto-level clouds are the ones I think of when it is overcast but it doesn't feel like rain is imminent. Those are the ones where I'm not quite sure if I should take an umbrella or not.

Altocumulus clouds are midlevel stratocumuliform clouds. They often form from cirrocumulus thickening and lowering in the sky. They have a rowlike structure of the cumulus shapes that can appear as fish scales. This lowering and thickening is a clue that a warm front or occluded front is approaching

Another personal favorite phrase describing altocumulus is the "buttermilk sky" because it reminds us of the curdled look of buttermilk. Other people describe it as the sheep cloud because the shapes reminded people in parts of Europe of the look of a herd of sheep grazing in the sky. These clouds even inspired modern composers like Hoagy Carmichael who composed "Ole Buttermilk Sky."

Altostratus clouds are midlevel clouds that create an overcast sky without much obvious structure to the clouds. Sometimes they are thin enough to see the light of the sun or moon through them and often they can be accompanied by a series of colorful rings called a corona. This optical effect is similar to the ring around the moon, but the light is diffracted by liquid water instead of ice. The corona is usually a series of pastel-colored rings circling the sun or moon. It is different than the single ring caused by the ice crystals of the cirrostratus but just as beautiful.

Low Clouds

The lowest clouds are the ones I think of when I look outside and think that rain or snow is coming soon. Stratus clouds are the gray overcast sky I often think of on gloomy days. The rain or snow is on its way but not happening yet. *Stratus* means "layers," so these low clouds layer over the sky, blocking out the sun and blue sky.

Once the rain or snow starts, the clouds are nimbostratus, with the prefix *nimbo-* meaning precipitation of some kind is falling from the clouds. Nimbostratus clouds can often appear dark and foreboding but are not usually associated with stormy activity.

Vertically Developing Clouds

The last general category of clouds is the vertically developing clouds, the ones that cross through more than one layer of the troposphere. The familiar cumulus cloud and its larger cousin the stormy cumulonimbus thunderhead are both in this family. These clouds build upward from convection, the energy they contain welling upward as the water vapor rises and changes its phase. This upwelling will be important to the life of these clouds. I will spend some time describing the cumulus and cumulonimbus in more detail in the chapter on storms.

There are many unusual cloud types too. Some only happen in certain geographical places; some only happen with very unusual and specific weather conditions. Examples include the beautiful lenticular clouds that form over the tops of mountains or the ominous mammatus clouds that foretell the potentially violent weather that spawns tornados.

ACTIVITY
Nephelomancy

Clouds have been used as divination tools for millennia. Nephelomancy, cloud divination, can be done as simply as looking at the shapes.[16] Maybe you did this as a child, looking up to see dragons or fire trucks or whatnot. I usually saw something to do with horses. When did you last look up at the clouds? Whatever your answer may be, it has likely been too long.

You will need
- a location to view clouds
- a notebook
- a writing instrument

Directions
Perform this work anytime there are clouds in the sky and conditions are safe to observe them.

The simplest way to perform cloud divination is to think of a question you want some insight on. Focus on that question as you look at the clouds. Try to not expect an outcome; simply let the shapes speak to your intuition. Make notes of the appearance, the direction of movement,

---

16.   Webster, *Llewellyn's Complete Book of Divination*, 84.

the altitude of the clouds. You might want to sketch or photograph the clouds as well.

Look at the shapes and see what images are revealed to you, and consider how they allow you to better understand your situation.

- Do you see a face, the shape of a creature, or another familiar shape?
- What importance do these images have to you?
- Which direction are the clouds moving in? Are they moving fast or slow?
- Are they high elevation or low?

Observe the clouds as they morph and change shapes over time, paying attention to the sequence of the images.

Make note of any impression you get in your notebook, describing what meaning you give to the different observations, and as you're studying your notes, reflect on how they give you insight into your question. If you don't have the ability to go outside and look at clouds, perhaps look for an online webcam or satellite image that shows cloud forms.

ACTIVITY
Create a Cloud Divination Tool

After you have used cloud divination for some time, you might want to create your own cloud divination tool, such as a deck, a set of glyphs or runes, or even a pendulum board.

You will need
- a notebook and writing instrument
- a set of cloud sketches/photos (optional)
- materials for whatever form of divination tool you wish to make

  Note: I will describe making a set of cloud glyphs on flat river stones then give some suggestions on how you might make a deck or a pendulum board.
- a permanent marker or paint pen (for stones)
- sealant for the paint

Directions

In your notebook, write down your divination system. Select the cloud forms you want to use. For each cloud, write down what your meaning will be. Include both an in-depth meaning as well as a few key words you can quickly recall.

I start out by ascribing meaning to the different types of clouds. For example, the wispy, light appearance of the cirrus clouds can mean happiness, lightheartedness, or wishes. Cumulus clouds, which are the ones often drawn by children, can represent carefree nature, joy, or childishness. The uniform overcast appearance of altostratus might imply stability, comfort, or prosperity.

The different cloud colors might provide meaning too: white clouds could be purification, protection, or a new beginning, whereas darker gray clouds might mean transforming from negative to positive energy, just like a gray candle can mean the same.

The different heights of the clouds could be about timing; for example, high clouds may mean the event is not happening right away, whereas low clouds could mean the timing is imminent. Heights could also have to do with the probability of something happening, with high clouds meaning a high probability and low clouds meaning the opposite.

The amount of cloud cover could also be interpreted as how clear a message is: if there are few clouds obscuring the sky, the answer is easy to see; if it is overcast, maybe that means the answer is not yet clear.

Select flat river stones large enough to easily put a symbol on. The glyphs I have used are simple line drawings of the cloud shapes. You can use that idea, or you can use your artistic talents and let your imagination run wild. Paint the glyph then seal the paint. Create a glyph for each cloud meaning.

After painting and sealing, you can use the stones for divination, which can be done several different ways. I do a single draw as a focus for the day. If I want more in-depth readings, I do a stone casting where I take my entire set of stones, dump them out on the table, then swirl them three times clockwise with my hand as I focus on what insight I hope to get from the reading. I look at how the stones group together, with any outliers or face-down stones not being part of the reading. I think about what meanings I have assigned to those clouds, then see how those meanings work together in that group. Another way I use my stones is like drawing cards. I draw multiple stones and lay them out in a reading.

Exercise extension

Making cloud cards could be as simple as printing out photos of clouds on cardstock and cutting them to the same size to make a deck. Laminating them would make them last longer. Drawing different cloud shapes in a circular pattern would make a good pendulum board. A simple way to make a board is to cut a six- to eight-inch-diameter circle from card stock and draw the cloud shapes around the outside edge, similar to numbers on a clock.

I like to use a pendulum made from a stone that is associated with weather energy; for example, I have a sunstone pendulum and a pendulum made from Arkansas quartz. Those are my go-to pendulums. I associate the sunstone with solar energy, which is the source of energy for weather, and Arkansas quartz is a great energy amplifier. As you hold the pendulum, focus on your question, then observe what shapes it moves over. Those cloud meanings will be the insight you are seeking.

CLOUD FORMATION

What causes this water vapor to rise in the troposphere? Air can be pushed up by a variety of factors, and the cooling of the air as it rises leads to the development of clouds. Knowing a bit more about this can make it easier to understand when and how clouds will form. Let's look at each one of these processes.

Local Convection

The first one is surface heating causing convection. This is the cause of the very predictable thunderstorms we would see many summer afternoons while we were in the hayfield. The sunlight would be absorbed by the earth's surface, causing it to heat up and creating "bubbles" of air at the surface called thermals. Maybe you have seen birds soaring along these thermals, enjoying the convection lifting them without them having to flap their wings.

As this bubble of air rises, it cools and begins to mix with the cooler, drier air around it. Much like in a lava lamp, more bubbles rise and bump into this mixed region, pushing it a little higher. If the rising air cools down to where it reaches its saturation point, the moisture condenses. Cool air has less capacity to store water vapor, and this saturation point depends on the humidity of the air carried on the thermal.

The condensation takes the form of a puffy cumulus cloud, specifically cumulus humilis. In the Ozarks, these afternoon puffballs were a common sight in the summer months. Many times, they would form and grow into cumulus congestus and towering cumulus, perhaps eventually forming that familiar thunderhead shape, the cumulonimbus. In very strong storms, you will sometimes see the pouchlike mammatus cloud that are formed from strong and turbulent convection. This strong convection is one of the hallmarks of a storm that might cause tornados.

We will talk more about storms in another chapter, so we will leave our cumulonimbus storm alone until then. For now, know that you could watch the cloud building up as the energy releases and see the puffy white mounds of ice crystals and the darker base of liquid water in them.

Orographic Lifting

Another way that air is forced upward is by the topography it is passing over. This is called orographic lifting. When air reaches a mountain range, it is forced up and over the top of the mountains. Again, the same cooling and condensing process happens, causing clouds to form on the windward slope of the mountains. Often the windward side is lovely, lush, and green. This lifting can cause the formation of the unusual lenticular clouds at the peaks of the mountains. Lenticular clouds sometimes even form in a way that they look like a stack of pancakes over the summit. These clouds have often been the source of their own lore and myths.

The leeward side is often referred to as the rain shadow on the mountain range. This is because the air loses most of its moisture due to it condensing as the air rises and cools over the mountains. This warm dry wind, sometimes called a Foehn wind, dries the vegetation. The Atacama Desert, purportedly the driest place on the planet, is in the rain shadow of the Andes. The American Dust Bowl occurred partly due to the warm, dry winds coming off the Rockies. The air coming down the leeward side heats as it moves lower and creates a warm, dry air mass. These localized winds like the Chinooks or Santa Anas have their own lore associated with them.

Convergence

The convergence of those global circulation cells at the surface also causes air to rise. The converging cells form a low-pressure system, and the air rising causes clouds to form from the cooling and condensation. One example is the ITCZ. The ITCZ looks like a band of clouds and showers, with an occasional thundershower, and is close to the equator. The position of the ITCZ isn't fixed but drifts northward or southward seasonally.

Frontal Uplift

The uplift along weather fronts is a final way that clouds can form. We talked about the cold and warm fronts and how they lift up the air to cause it to cool. Now we can look at the cloud patterns that will give us a hint about what front is coming, and we have a way to know ahead of time what weather is likely coming too.

EXERCISE
Cloud Energy Work

The energy stored in clouds is available to me for doing magical energy work. Using what I know about the type of cloud as well as its direction of motion enhances my energy work. For example, I use stratus clouds and their overcast appearance for protection work over my farm and to charge my wards on the property lines from a distance. Or I could use the wispy high cirrus clouds as a focal point for getting the "bigger picture" intuition on a situation, since from their high location, I would "see" more. Nimbostratus clouds might be my choice if I want to nourish a situation to grow or to wash the magical slate clean.

If I have a friend in need of supportive energy, I will use clouds that are moving in their direction to add an extra boost to the energy I am sending them. If the clouds aren't moving in the correct direction, I can still make use of their energy. Instead, I consider that direction's magical correspondences: colors, parts of the body, and other active and passive properties.[17]

You will need
- a location to view clouds where you will not be disturbed

---

17.   Morrison, *Craft*, 20–23.

Directions

The timing of this work can be based on the type of clouds and their direction of movement or when this work needs to be done. Here's one of my favorite quotes from Silver RavenWolf: "Besides, in such emergency cases who has time to run for red thread and start running around the kitchen table?"[18] If the work needs doing, do it.

Settle in your chosen location. Take a moment to clear your mind and ground yourself by taking a few deep breaths. Focus your mind on the person or situation you wish to do energy work for.

Visualize gathering a ball of energy between your hands. The color of the energy should be appropriate to whatever your work is focusing on. I use white for protection, green for healing, blue for calming, and yellow for joy. Use what feels right to you.

When you are ready, gaze skyward and choose the clouds you wish to send that energy to. Visualize the energy flowing from your glowing ball upward into the cloud, filling it with the color of the energy you are sending. After you have charged the cloud with the energy you gathered, repeat this three times:

Speed on cloud, be on your way
Be my messenger on this day
Take this gift to one dear to me
As I will, so mote it be

---

18. RavenWolf, *American Folk Magick*, 207.

Thank the cloud for being your messenger and release it on its way. Close out this work by drawing in any energy connections you might still have open. Ground yourself once more to complete the work.

If you are not in a place where you are able to see clouds directly, or you're unable to go outside, you could instead use a satellite image of the clouds in your area or even a photograph of a cloud if no other options are easily accessible.

Exercise extension

An extension of this exercise is to utilize not only the cloud but also the weather changes it is predicting to enhance your energy work. The cirrus and altocumulus clouds predict coming rain and warmer temperatures, whereas cumulonimbus often precede a cold front. You could use the temperature changes as a boost for your energy work, cooling off or warming up a situation perhaps.

CRAFT
Make Your Own Felt Cumulus Cloud

Now that you know the lore about what weather these clouds foretell, you can use that as part of your energy work. If you want to carry a little cloud energy with you all the time, there are plenty of adorable DIY patterns to craft yourself a little cloud as well as books that can give you more magical ideas for your cloud.[19] As a fiber crafter and sewist, I can think of many ways I could make a cloud

---

19.   Luna, *Fiber Magick*, 19–27.

form that I could use in my practice. If nothing else, the tried-and-true craft many of us did in primary school with construction paper and cotton balls will work.

I believe all magic is local, so if I can make something with my own hands, it will be just as useful as any other tool I have at my disposal. This may seem a very simple craft, but remember, it's about the intention, energy, or will you put into your craft as you make it. That's where the magic lies!

You will need

- white felt and a fabric pencil
- fabric scissors
- a cloud pattern
- white thread or fabric glue to attach cloud pieces together
- sewing needle (if sewing cloud pieces together)
- pattern/directions for your cloud
- straight pins or clips for holding the cloud shapes together while sewing (optional)
- stuffing
- extra magical goodies (dried herbs, small crystals, charms, beads) to add to stuffing or to embellish (optional)

Directions

The timing here is anytime you are feeling crafty, but as with other things, you might choose a magical timing if you have a particular intent for your cloud.

Figure 7: Cloud Pattern

If I want to add magical intent to this, I focus on the purpose of my cloud as I create it. I even write a spell to add extra magic as I sew it up.

Trace then cut out cloud pattern pieces. Place the pieces on white felt and cut out two cloud shapes (front and back). If you are using patterned felt, you will need mirror images, but plain felt doesn't require this. If sewing the pieces together, carefully pin or clip the front to the back, wrong sides together.

Be sure to leave about an inch open for stuffing and sew the pieces together about a fourth to half an inch from the edge of the felt. Space stitches close together so any goodies you put inside don't fall out. (If you prefer to use glue instead of sewing, also leave about an inch open.)

As you sew, recite the following:

> *Happy cloud, floating by*
> *Bless my world from on high*
> *Happy cloud, floating free*

Carrying good energy
Happy cloud, floating soft
Carry my wishes aloft
Happy cloud, floating free
As I will, so mote it be

Lightly stuff the cloud, including any herbs or crystals if you choose. Sew up (or glue) the opening. Embellish if desired.

Keep your cloud around you when you want a little extra boost of energy. I keep mine in my desk at work and another smaller one in my car.

FOG AND MIST

Fog and mist are both due to water vapor condensing and are used interchangeably but there is a difference between them. Mist and fog are both droplets that are so small they get suspended in the air, sort of like a cloud on the ground.

Fog is essentially a cloud settling on the ground due to its density, while mist is held near the ground by a layer of cooler air above it. Fog often forms over bodies of water on cool mornings after a period of warm days. The warm water evaporates into the air and almost immediately condenses as it rises because of the cooler temperatures. Another difference between fog and mist is how much visibility there is. Fog has low visibility, usually less than a thousand meters, while mist has greater visibility.

ACTIVITY
Fog Ancestor Meditation

Fog or mist is sometimes viewed as a liminal space. I remember many stories that involved finding a fairy-tale land or magical place after walking through a fog or mist. Using a foggy morning as a time for meditation or ancestor work might open unexpected channels of communication. Of course, you want to make sure you have done your due diligence on energy hygiene and don't just go off willy-nilly here. Being properly prepared spiritually, mentally, and physically for this kind of work is essential.

You will need
- a quiet place to sit and meditate
- fog
- ancestor offering items (optional, but I was raised to never show up at someone's home empty-handed!)
- candles, incense, crystals to help you focus (optional)
- a notebook and a writing instrument to record any thoughts or impressions (optional)

Directions
Timing of this work should be when there is fog present.

Create your meditation space using your preferred method. If you typically cast a circle, now is the time to do that. If you have other rituals you use to call upon your ancestors, perform those as well. I usually place a cup of very strong black coffee and a piece of tobacco out if I want to call upon my grandpa, for example.

After preparing your meditation space, settle in and clear your mind. Take a few deep breaths to focus on the work at hand. Visualize reaching a tendril of energy out through the fog to the realms of your ancestors. You may choose to recite a prayer or invocation for them. I generally use one from *Badass Ancestors.*[20]

As you feel their energy and yours make contact, feel them sending you blessings and protection. Let this feeling surround you like the fog that swirls around you. Spend time feeling the fog suffuse this energy into you. Once you feel your work is done, thank your ancestors and release them back to their realm.

Perform your preferred rituals of closing your meditation space, leaving behind any offers if it is safe to do so. Record any thoughts or impression of the meditation if you choose.

Exercise extension

An adaptation of this is to use the fog to surround yourself or another person with healing or protective energy. Instead of calling upon ancestors, imagine imbuing the fog with the energy that surrounds the person so they have it available to tap into. Also, since fog obscures things, I will use it to make the energies undetectable to those who might wish them harm. I use this concept a lot when I or a loved one is traveling. I want them to be visible to traffic for sure, but if someone wants to mug them, I visualize the fog as protecting them.

---

20. Wigington, *Badass Ancestors*, 103–126.

If it isn't foggy the day you want to do these meditations, I would instead choose a stone that reminds me of fog, for example, a smoky quartz. Ideally, I would have allowed this crystal to sit out in fog prior to needing it for magical work. I would perform the meditation work as above, just using the smoky quartz as my focal point instead of the fog.

WEATHER LORE

It turns out that a good bit of the weather lore surrounding clouds does accurately predict the weather within reason. Also, it seems that cloud weather lore is among the most widely known and quoted. I remember listening to the old farmers at the feedstore talking about the ring around the moon or the mackerel sky when I was a kid following my dad and grandpa around. Farmers are some of the best observational scientists I know because their livelihood is so intimately tied to the weather.

Ring around the moon, rain or snow by noon.

The ring around the moon is caused by cirrostratus clouds. These clouds are so high and thin they are difficult to see during the day. The sunlight is too bright for us to see them. At night, the moonlight will show these beautiful clouds. The moonlight will scatter off the ice crystals in these high thin clouds, and from our point of view on the ground this will give us a view of a glowing ring.

That ring around the moon tells us that a weather front is on the way! Remember that cirrostratus clouds precede all the weather fronts we talked about. Depending on the front type, it can lead them by twelve to twenty-four hours. All the fronts bring precipitation, so we can expect rain or snow in the next day or so. Now, some folks say the number of stars inside the ring can tell you how many inches of rain or snow are coming. Unfortunately, that piece of lore has no science backing it up. It's just chance what stars are in the sky near the moon that night; they don't give us any clues about the weather coming.

> *The circle of the moon never filled a pond.*
> *The circle of the sun wets a shepherd.*

This is an extension of the ring around the moon. The cirrostratus clouds often mean a cold front is coming, so the rain will be stormy and fast and won't fill the pond. The altostratus clouds that cause the ring around the sun mean a warm front, which might mean prolonged rain.

This lore could also pertain to coronae around the sun or moon. A corona is a series of colored rings around the moon or sun. The moon or sun's disk of light is visible through the obscuring clouds, but it isn't as sharp or clear as when a ring forms. A corona also extends out from the disk of the moon or sun rather than being some distance from it as with a ring. Coronae are formed when the cloud is composed of droplets of similar size so are generally associated with altocumulus or cirrocumulus clouds or even fog. These clouds usually precede fronts that have gentle but short-lived rain.

> *Trace in the sky a painter's brush,*
> *the winds around you will soon rush.*

Another version is "the clouds called goat's hair or gray mares' tails forbodes wind." The cirrus clouds, with their wispy look of a painter's brush, precede all the weather fronts. Remember, the fronts all bring a change in the wind and weather, so the wind change will be noticeable. The cirrus clouds by themselves don't tell you exactly what kind of front is coming, but you can pair that with the temperature, the wind direction change, and the next clouds that appear to figure out what the weather will be.

Mackerel sky, mackerel sky,
never long wet, never long dry.

Altocumulus clouds often have the broken and scaly appearance that reminds us of fish scales. These clouds often get called a mackerel sky. So, this saying comes from these clouds appearing about six to twelve hours before the arrival of the rains or snow of a warm front or an occluded front. Another version of this is "if clouds look as if scratched by a hen, get ready to reef your topsails in."

Put them together and you get "mares' tails and mackerel scales make lofty ships carry low sails." The cirrus clouds are the mares' tails and the mackerel scales are the altocumulus clouds. They tell you that showers and maybe some thundershowers are on the way.

The higher the clouds, the better the weather.

Now that we know cirrus clouds often presage storm fronts, we know this isn't always the case. If we consider only the puffy, happy cumulus clouds, this can work to a degree. However, now we know that those turn into cumulonimbus by vertically developing, so even then it's a stretch to make it work.

The fox is brewing.

This saying of German origin describes mist that lingers over brooks and meadows after sunset. This often foretells good weather since that means there is cooler air above these places. Because cool air holds less moisture, it is usually associated with good weather.

In the morning, mountains;
in the afternoon, fountains.

This piece of lore ties into storm development, which we will talk about in a later chapter. To tie it to cloud forms, the tall forms of the cumulonimbus or cumulus congestus clouds can be compared to mountains. If those clouds are in your area, you can almost certainly count on hard, stormy rain.

When clouds look like black smoke,
a wise man puts on a cloak.

Liquid water absorbs light rather than reflecting it as ice does. Clouds or parts of clouds that contain liquid water will look dark to an observer on the ground. These dark clouds could definitely be bringing rain, so time for a raincoat!

A summer fog for fair, a winter fog for rain.
A fact most everywhere, in valley or on plain.

For a summer fog to form, usually it requires a clear night for the temperatures to drop to the dewpoint. So, a clear night usually foretells a nice day to follow. On the other hand, a winter fog is formed when warm air from a warm front moves over a cold area. The temperature drops in the warm air creating fog, but the moisture will likely bring rain along with it.

This is seemingly contradicted by the French saying "fog that rises in autumn portends the beautiful weather; fog rising in summer announces rain." The fog in summer could be due to a cold front moving over warmer water causing the fog in valleys or near waterways. The autumn fog could be due to warm air moving over colder water, predicting a mild period approaching.

> *When the clouds are green and black,*
> *they forbode storms and lightning.*

This Italian saying is describing the dark, liquid-laden nimbo clouds. These can often be part of the cumulonimbus clouds that are the form thunderstorms take on.

> *If woolly fleeces spread the heavenly way,*
> *be sure no rain disturbs the summer's day.*

This phrase describes the fluffy cumulus clouds that are also called fair-weather cumulus. They are often associated with fair weather.

> *When the sun sets with a hat on,*
> *that foretells wet weather for the morrow.*

This French saying does have some truth in it for most of the midlatitudes. If there are clouds in the west, there could be a weather system on the way.

WINDING IT UP

Understanding the science of clouds encouraged me to look once again to the sky with wonder. Not only do I see the shapes of a dragon or sailboat, I see a source of magical inspiration and energy. Clouds can predict the future using science and folklore, so now I can add magic to that bag of tricks as well.

Now that you know more about the science of clouds in all their forms, how can you use that information in your energy work? Maybe start with a cloud journal, creating your own divination system. Maybe use fog in your ancestor or protection work. What other ways could you imagine using clouds and their cousins, fog and dew, in your practice?

Chapter 6
RAIN
Nourishing the Earth

Rain is the lifeblood to living things on Earth. Water is essential for life, so much so that when looking at extrasolar planets, one of the first things that is looked for is evidence of liquid water or water ice in the atmosphere of the planet.[21]

Water is also a key element in many different practices. Water being essential to life gives it extra importance magically. Also, since it is often tied to emotional well-being and love, it is one of the elements that comes up frequently when people start their metaphysical journey. Understanding that water in nature carries tremendous energy makes my magical practice more potent.

THE WATER CYCLE

Rain is a key part of the water cycle on Earth, and since I'm a witch who loves cycles, let's talk about it. The water cycle is the continuous movement of water on the earth and through its atmosphere.

---

21. Witze, "Earth-Sized Planet," 381–382.

In grade school science, you may have learned it consists of three parts: evaporation, condensation, and precipitation.

Figure 8: The Water Cycle

Liquid water evaporates forming water vapor, then it condenses into clouds and eventually will fall as precipitation in the form of rain or snow. That covers the basics of the water cycle, but, of course, reality is more complex than that. Particularly, scientists still don't have a full understanding of all the journeys water takes as it moves through vegetation and the geology of

Earth's surface. For my purposes, I will just stick to the simpler version. Previous chapters talked about the first two steps, evaporation and condensation. These next two chapters will look at precipitation.

Rain Formation

There are two processes that form rain, depending on the latitude of the location. Raindrops need a condensation nucleus to form. Even on a clear day there are all sorts of microscopic particles in the air. These little particles provide a surface for the water droplets to condense on. They can be particles of pollen, dust, or salt, particles from smoke, or plumes from volcanoes. All that magic hiding inside that raindrop! How amazing!

At the latitudes of the continental United States, the primary process is the collision-coalescence process. To have this happen, larger droplets form around some of the larger, but still relatively speaking very tiny, condensation nuclei. These larger droplets are crucial to increasing the chances that a collision will happen.

These droplets will start to fall because, as in most things, gravity eventually wins, but the air resistances slows the fall. As the particle grows, there is a balancing act between the downward pull of gravity and the increasing air resistance, but the larger drops will usually fall faster than the smaller ones. This allows the particle to gather even more smaller cloud droplets and grow in size.

The thicker the clouds, the longer it takes the droplets to finally make their way out of the cloud. In some cases, it can take a droplet close to an hour to finally fall out of the cloud as precipitation! Drizzle, on the other hand, often comes from stratus clouds because they are comparatively thin clouds, so the droplets don't have as much time to grow before reaching the bottom of the cloud.

This air resistance is also what gives the droplets their shape as they fall. Sadly, I'm about to burst your bubble—rain is not "raindrop" shaped. The shapes, based on the volume of the drop, are like hamburger buns, spherical, or almost flat like pancakes. Eventually the drop becomes too large, and it is pulled apart by the air resistance. Drops are mostly smaller than a few millimeters. This compares to the tip of a typical ink pen in size. I know, science takes away our fun again, but nature loves efficiency, and this is the most efficient way for drops to fall.

The other way rain forms occurs at higher latitudes, or in the tall cumulonimbus clouds year-round, or during the colder months at middle latitudes where the freezing level of the clouds is closer to the ground. These colder conditions mean more of the cloud is above this freezing level. The cloud droplets form in a similar way as I described before, but in these colder clouds something interesting happens. The water cools below the temperature that it's supposed to freeze at, but it doesn't freeze! This is still liquid water even though it's below its freezing point, so it is said to be "supercooled."

The ice particles that are interspersed in the supercooled liquid drops act as the condensation point for the drops. The ice crystals form around the condensation nuclei, but in this environment some of the crystals form as ice immediately through a sort of flash-freezing process when they contact the cold nuclei.

Without getting too far into the weeds about saturation vapor pressure, I'll just say that it is higher close to the supercooled liquid drop than it is close to the ice particle. Mother Nature doesn't like an imbalance, so water vapor molecules that were hanging out near the liquid drop begin to move toward the ice crystal. Eventually even molecules that were originally part of the drop will diffuse away toward the ice crystal. This exchange is called the Bergeron process.

The drop evaporates with liquid transferring to vapor then moving and the crystal grows by deposition. Deposition is a phase change most of us have never heard of even though it does happen around us. Deposition is where vapor goes directly to a solid. It is the reverse of the sublimation process that dry ice will go through when it goes straight from solid to gas in my spooky Samhain decorations! Water vapor deposits on the ice crystal as a solid, so the drop gets smaller and the ice crystal gets bigger.

You may ask yourself, "Why is she talking about ice crystals when this is supposed to be about rain?" Well, once the ice crystal gets big enough, again that pesky gravity wins, and the crystal starts to fall. If it passes the freezing line in the cloud, it will melt, and the ice crystal becomes a raindrop, and it continues its journey down as rain.

Virga is caused by rain that falls through dry air, and so the rain evaporates before it has a chance to hit the ground. These showers look almost like streamers unfurling from the bottom of the cloud.

ACTIVITY
Gathering Rainwater for Magical Use

Water is a key component in so many forms of magical work. So why not use rainwater instead of tap water? I capture rainwater for use on my farm already, and sad to say it took me a surprisingly long time before I made the leap to collecting it for my magical use. Right now, I'm talking about rainwater in general, but in a later chapter I'll talk about thunderstorm water.

You will need

- an outdoor location to collect rainwater
- a container to collect water in
- incense or other materials to cleanse container
- cheesecloth or muslin to strain water
- a storage container for water

Directions

Before the rain arrives, use your preferred method to energetically cleanse your collection container. I use a heavy-duty plastic mixing bowl, so I wash it with seawater.

Place it in a safe location. Wait for the rain to arrive so it can collect rainwater. Bring the collection container inside. Carefully strain collected water through fabric to remove any plant matter that might have blown into it; this is to prevent mold from forming. Store strained water in your preferred storage container. I like to label and date my container.

You can use this water as you would any water in your magical practice. I use it in my healing bowl. I can add it to a spray bottle with oils or stones to use as a general altar and tool cleansing spray. I even save some of the rainwater I collect for ritual baths.

Exercise extension

An extension of this activity is to collect water at special times. I pay attention for the opportunity to collect rain that falls on "auspicious days": a sabbat, a feast day, a day of the week ascribed to a deity I work with, my birthday, and so on. Using rain collected on special days or times gives it that extra boost of added energy. Rain gathered on a special day or in a special container is my preferred water to use in my scrying bowl. If I am wanting to focus on work-related issues, for example, I might choose rain gathered on Sunday for help with success or weather or on Thursday for abundance and prosperity. The same could be true for using rainwater in energy work. I would choose rain captured on a day of the week that would most help achieve my intended goal.

CRAFT
Chakra Stone Rain Chain

Remember, rainwater can be used in any of the ways you would use water in your practice. It just gives a little extra boost since it's straight from Mother Nature. A good way to collect rainwater is to use a rain chain. Rain chains are a simple but decorative way to direct water into a container. Of course, there are plenty of purveyors of fine goods who would happily sell you a rain chain, but why not make one of your own?

My instructions below are a mash-up of several I have found plus my own twist of using stones that are aligned to the seven chakras. The stones I list are ones that are typically found either at your local metaphysical shop or from vendors at a witchy or metaphysical event.

You will need

- 20-gauge wire (3 to 4 times the length you want your finished chain to be)

- needle-nose pliers for cutting and wrapping
- stones that represent the chakras (the amount you need will depend on the length of the chain—I recommend 3 to 4 stones per foot of finished length)
- a tray or towel to lay stones out in order
- a saltwater bath to cleanse the stones

Note: Here are some possible chakra stones.[22]

Root	Sacral	Solar Plexus	Heart	Throat	Third Eye	Crown
Obsidian	Carnelian	Tiger's Eye	Aventurine	Amazonite	Opalite	Clear Quartz
Tuxedo Jasper	Orange Calcite	Aragonite	Emerald	Sodalite	Lapis Lazuli	Howlite
Smoky Quartz	Red Jasper	Picture Jasper	Green Jade	Blue Calcite	Fluorite	Amethyst

Directions

You can make this craft anytime, but if you want to add extra energy boosts to it, you can work on a particular day of the week, on an auspicious day, during a particular moon phase, or any timing that has significance to you.

Start by giving the stones a good physical and energetic cleansing in a saltwater bath. Lay the stones out on the tray or towel in the order you want them in your chain.

Individually wire-wrap the stones, placing a joining loop of wire at the top and bottom of each stone except for the bottom stone. Connect the stones in your desired order by wiring the joining loops together until you have completed your chain.

---

22. Simmons and Ahsian, *Book of Stones*, XXVII–XXX.

Hang your chain from a location that receives direct rainfall, making sure the bottom of your chain directs the rain into your collection device or the area you want the rain to go to.

Craft extension

Work on your chain as you do a chakra-related meditation to imbue even more energy into the rain as it passes over the stones. If you would rather work with ancestor energy, instead of stones, make a rain chain from old teacups or cutlery. There are really no rules about what a rain chain can be made from as long as it directs the rain downward along it.

DROUGHT

A natural extension of talking about rain is to talk about drought. Drought is broadly defined as a period of abnormally dry weather for a region usually lasting longer than a season. This is different than a predictable dry spell that occurs regularly in a region, say the dry period in the desert Southwest when the monsoon season reverses. Droughts happen periodically in most climates around the world, but due to climate change, they are becoming harder to predict and more extreme.

There are different types of droughts, but for my purposes, I will focus on the type caused by a lack of precipitation in an area. This can happen for a variety of meteorological reasons, such as strong high-pressure systems moving into an area and not dissipating. Another cause can be a prevalence of continental winds that are dry, decreasing the humidity in an area. These two factors can suppress the formation of thunderstorms or prevent a rain system from moving into an area. Once drought conditions are established, heating can cause even more water loss through evaporation.

There are long-term patterns such as El Niño and La Niña that can create drought conditions in an area. Movement of the ITCZ, the band of low pressure near the equator, away from an area can increase the chances for drought. There is mounting evidence that climate change is contributing to drought conditions particularly in the developing world.[23] These three factors not only create drought conditions in some areas, but they can also bring monsoon or flooding conditions to other areas.

Drought can have a devastating impact on the agriculture and ecosystems of the area where it is occurring. Water tables can drop, crops will fail, and livestock and wildlife will die. In severe drought conditions, there is an increased risk of wildfires from dead vegetation and dust storms from winds carrying dry soil aloft. The Dust Bowl in the Great Plains in the 1930s was due to an extended period of drought coupled with poor farming practices. Millions of lives were impacted by these conditions.

EXERCISE
Rain Gauge Spell

The rain gauge spell is essentially the reverse of burning a candle down. Obviously, rain is less predictable than burning a candle, but for water energy, I love using this for long-term work that doesn't need urgent action.

You will need

- a rain gauge
- a notebook and writing instrument

---

23. Dai, "Drought Under Global Warming," 45–65.

Directions

Timing of this work should be when there is rain in the forecast. If you are wanting to use the entire gauge, you may need multiple rain events to complete this work.

To start this work, count the number of major marks on the rain gauge (typically an inch in the United States). The number of marks can be used to time your spell work or if you are doing a working that has multiple steps. Label the list in your notebook.

Watch as the rain fills the gauge, marking off the stages as it fills over time. Once the gauge reaches the top mark you are using or is full, the spell is done. Pour the water out in a safe location or on a plant that might benefit from the energy raised in the spell work.

ACTIVITY
Seed Spell

Rain nourishes plants for growth, giving them life and energy, so using seed planting and rain to manifest seems a natural next step.

You will need

- seeds
- a seed-starting medium
- seed-starting trays or pots
- biodegradable paper
- a nontoxic writing instrument
- collected magical rainwater

Directions

The timing of this work needs to correspond to the growing season of whatever seed you choose.

Write a word or two about the intent or goal of your spell on the paper and prepare the seed-starting medium and pot for planting. Using your finger, make a hole of the appropriate size for planting your seed in the medium. Coil the paper with your words around your finger. Fit the paper inside the hole. Place the seed in the hole surrounded by the paper. Fill in the hole with the soil.

As you water the seed with your collected rainwater, focus on the intent of your spell and imagine the rainwater adding its energy to your work. Repeat the following three times:

Rainwater, nourish this seed
Give it energy that it needs
As this seed does surely grow
My desire manifests also

Each time the seed or seedling needs to be watered, use your rainwater and repeat this process until you are ready to plant the seedling outside.

RAINBOWS

Now is a good time to talk about rainbows. Rainbows have captured human imagination pretty much as long as there have been humans. Certainly, many cultures and paths have stories about the significance of rainbows. I think that understanding how rainbows form from a scientific perspective only serves to enhance their beauty and magic.

Physics of Rainbow Formation

To understand how rainbows form, I need to talk about light. Light travels at different speeds in different materials. It travels fastest in the vacuum of space, it slows down slightly in air, and it slows down even more in water. This causes the path the light is traveling on to change direction as it moves from one medium to another, which is called refraction.

Now, the reverse will also cause a change in speed. The speed of the light will increase as it travels from the water into the air. This also causes the path to change. It turns out in cases where the light speeds up as it enters a new material, there is a possibility of a different phenomenon occurring where the light doesn't enter the new material at all. Total internal reflection occurs when the light's path bends so much as it tries to refract into the new material that it actually reflects off the boundary and bounces back into the material it is in. This doesn't happen all the time at the boundary, just for light coming in at a large enough angle (think slanted, not head-on to the boundary). Total internal reflection is what gives faceted gemstones their sparkles and why fiber optic cables work.

The last piece of the puzzle needed to understand rainbows is the phenomenon of dispersion. If you hang pretty crystals in your window to make rainbows, you are already a fan of dispersion. Remember, a rainbow is a mixture of colors: ROYGBIV. This is the mnemonic for remembering the colors in white light. Sunlight has this mix of colors: red, orange, yellow, green, blue, indigo, and violet. In chapter 1, I described pulling out these different colors to charge tools and use them for other energy work.

There is another way to separate out the colors of light. As it turns out, when white light enters some material, in this case water, there are different "speed limits" for different colors of light. Red light slows down less than the blue light, so the colors fan out because each one's path is at a slightly different angle. This fanning out of the different colors is dispersion.

Now I have all the pieces of the puzzle to talk about how rainbows form. The conditions needed to see a rainbow include the sun and rain clouds being opposite one another in the sky, and the sun has to be relatively close to the horizon, not directly overhead. To be able to see a potential rainbow, I should stand with the sun at my back, facing toward the clouds. The light from the sun will hit the raindrops in the clouds, passing from the air into the water. Two things happen at this point: the light slows down, causing the path to change, and the light disperses into the different colors.

The light keeps traveling away from me in the raindrop until the light gets to the other side of the drop where once again there is a boundary, this time going from water to air. This is the place where total internal reflection can happen if the light is coming in at a large enough angle. If this does happen, the dispersed light is reflected back toward me, and I get to see a rainbow!

Now each droplet of rain reflects a particular color that depends on the angle of viewing, so the red in the rainbow is coming from different drops than the violet. As the sun's angle changes eventually, the ability to have total internal reflection goes away and the rainbow disappears.

In some situations, the angle is right for some of the raindrops to totally internally reflect the light twice before it exits back toward the viewer. The geometry of this second reflection will cause the color order to reverse. The light also becomes less intense since it is split off twice, with some being reflected and some refracting out of the raindrop in the way it was headed. This is the condition for a double rainbow to form. The secondary bow will be dimmer and the color order will be reversed from the primary bow.

The bow shape comes from the fact that the rainbow is a segment of a circle and would be circular if it formed in its entirety. How much of the bow I'm able to see depends on several factors. The lower the sun is in the sky, the more of the bow's arc is visible. If the sun is at the horizon opposite the clouds, I could potentially see half a circle of arc! Sometimes there are not enough raindrops in the right position or the position of the sun in the sky means the earth blocks part of the arc.

Other Types of Bows

Moonlight can also form rainbows; they are just not as bright. The full moon is many orders of magnitude dimmer than the sun. The moonbows are formed in the same way from a physics perspective as a regular rainbow. Because the light is so much dimmer, moonbows appear colorless. This is not due to the physics, but rather to the biological limitations of the human eye. The parts of the human eye responsible for color vision don't function in dim light, so the colors don't appear. One way to see the colors of a moonbow is to take a long-exposure photograph.

Fog can form bows for similar reasons, but because the droplet size in fog is so small, the light doesn't get a chance to disperse like it does in the larger raindrops. Therefore, fog bows look colorless. These bows will appear when the fogbank is beginning to clear, allowing the sunlight to be visible as it hits the droplets.

Understanding the science of rainbows doesn't take away their magic and beauty. In fact, to me, knowing that it takes these very specific conditions to create them makes them even more amazing. I hope it gives you even more appreciation of them too!

EXERCISE
Rainbow Chakra Exercise

If you work with chakra energies, you could try the following exercise. If you want more information on the chakras, there are several resources available, but I particularly like the information presented in *Elemental Witchcraft*.[24] Note that this meditation could be done just using sunlight, but if you could happen to time it when there is a rainbow in the sky, even better!

Some of the properties I associate with the chakras:

Root (Red): grounding, physical identity, security
Sacral (Orange): sexuality, pleasure, creativity
Solar Plexus (Yellow): self-confidence, self-esteem
Heart (Green): love, compassion
Throat (Blue): communication, self-talk
Third Eye (Indigo): intuition, thoughts, imagination
Crown (Violet): spiritual self, cosmic connection,
    awareness

You will need
- a comfortable location
- a notebook and writing instrument

Directions
Choose a comfortable location outside and face the rainbow if possible. Make sure the storm is far enough away to no longer be a danger. If the sun is out, be sure to wear sunscreen.

---

24. Michelle, *Elemental Witchcraft*, 150–151.

Visualize the colors from the rainbow passing through the air and scan the chakra center that corresponds to each color. Feel the light filling up the chakra centers, topping up and restoring their energy. As you feel that the light of the rainbow has finished its work, visualize the energy cords detaching and returning to the cloud the rainbow is in.

Sit for a few moments, feeling the energetic recharge and balance of your chakras. Write down any thoughts or impressions in your notebook.

Exercise extension

I realize that doing this meditation in real time with a rainbow could prove very tricky, so I will offer you this alternative. Select stones that correspond to the chakras. For example, aventurine works well for the heart (fourth) chakra.[25] When a mid- to late-afternoon storm is predicted, you could lay your stones out so that if a rainbow forms, they could soak up its energy. Then you could use these stones to benefit from the rainbow energy. For ideas which stones to choose, you can look back at the chakra rain chain craft (page 120) for a partial list.

If you are organized enough, you could place your tools out to bathe in the light of the rainbow. Since rainbows are ephemeral, you don't have much time to get yourself together for this. If you do make the effort, the synchronicity of the conditions needed to make a rainbow imparts an added energy boost to the tools. Position and timing are key, so rainbows can give your tools that boost of "right place at the right time" energy. I especially like to use rainbow energy to bless or cleanse my boline and

---

25. Simmons and Ahsian, *Book of Stones*, 56–57.

other curved blades, such as my vintage herb chopping knife.

Another extension could be using the rainbow for divination or meditation. Some traditions hold that rainbows are the path of souls to the afterlife, so they are a way to send messages to those who have crossed over.[26] Simply sitting and meditating or focusing on the rainbow might be a good practice to add to your ancestor work. For those with the gift of contacting the departed, this might also help enhance or strengthen that connection.

Rainbows would be a good thing to incorporate in work for good fortune or good luck. I meditate or do magical work for guidance or as a check-in to make sure I am headed in the right direction. If I happen to see a rainbow in that same time frame, I will take it as a positive sign confirming I am headed in the right direction.

WEATHER LORE

Certainly, knowing when rain is coming ahead of time is a useful skill. If you are a farmer, reading the signs in the sky would let you know when to plant or harvest your crops. Sailors would want to know if rain was coming in case they needed to harvest drinking water. Even people planning outdoor events would benefit from being able to know what weather is headed their way. As an avid hiker and trail rider, I pay attention to rain-related weather lore when I am planning to hit the trails. As a witch, I also pay attention so I can plan my magical work centered around rain more effectively.

---

26. Sterk, *Indigenous Cultural Translation*, 68.

When dew is on the grass,
rain will never come to pass.

Dew forms on the grass when the temperature of the air cools enough to reach the dewpoint temperature. This happens in a similar process to what we talked about earlier with the rising air cooling, but the cooling usually happens overnight. The water vapor condenses out of the air and collects on various surfaces. Usually this only happens on clear nights when the temperature can drop quicker.

The clear conditions that form the dew mean it likely won't rain soon after sunrise. *Never* is a bit of a strong word since obviously storm systems can move in after the dew forms, certainly bringing rain. But generally, this bit of lore is true in the short term.

The dews of the evening industriously shun;
they are the tears of the night for the loss of the sun.

This Scots proverb is a caution against collecting the dew formed at evening time. There is no correlation to any weather event except that the air would be cooling down rapidly at night.

The related saying "when grass is dry by morning light, look for rain before the night" corresponds to the dew not forming overnight since temperatures didn't drop enough due to persistent cloud cover. Again, this may be somewhat or conditionally correct, although there may be other reasons the dew didn't form other than it having been cloudy. Strong breezes can prevent dew forming, so those might also herald rain, or they might not!

Clear moon,
frost soon.

Frost is the frozen cousin to dew. When the moisture condenses out of the air and comes in contact with surfaces at or below freezing, frost will form. Remember, clouds act like thermal insulation, keeping heat in. A cloudless night, one that allows for more cooling, will be more conducive to frost forming. Another saying related to this is "cold is the night when the stars shine bright."

When fog falls, fair weather follows;
when it rises, rain ensues.

This piece of lore actually does have some scientific validity. Even though I discussed fog in the previous chapter, I think this one fits in here nicely following the discussion of rainfall. Falling or sinking air indicates that there is high pressure over an area. High pressure is associated with fair weather, so that works! Rising air usually indicates a low-pressure system, so that could mean storms are on the way. A more unusual version of that is "when fog goes up the mountain, you may go hunting; when it comes down the mountain, you may go fishing." The fog is sometimes pushed upslope by the sinking air, creating fair weather for the hunter. The rising air of the low pressure will allow the fog to roll into the valley, and there is some evidence that fish bite better when a low-pressure system is moving into an area. These sayings are tying rain back to high- and low-pressure systems as well as to fog.

When sound travels far and wide,
a stormy day will betide.

This is another saying I always found interesting. Sound travels at different speeds in different materials. That is why our voices sound funny if we inhale helium or sound distorted underwater.

The denser the medium, the faster sound will travel through it. Humid air is more dense than dry air, so sound travels faster and thus farther when the air is more humid, so that could mean rain is on its way.

My favorite version of the above lore is "when the forest murmurs and the mountains roar, close your windows and shut your doors." It seems there are two parts to this saying. The sounds traveling as described above is part of it. The other part is the wind picking up, causing the trees and leaves to move about. Mountain valleys can often act as wind tunnels, causing the sound to be amplified into a roar. A side note: one of my favorite sounds is the wind blowing through the pine trees in my cattle pasture.

Three days rain will empty any sky.

This piece of lore can generally be regarded as true. Most weather systems don't linger over an area for an extended period. They will clear out of an area within a few days. However, if the rain is part of a stationary front, all bets are off!

A rainbow in the morning gives you fair warning.
A rainbow afternoon, good weather coming soon.

This piece of lore works pretty well for my latitude since "rainbow in the morning" would mean rainbows appear in the west. This means that rain is to the west, and since the weather here generally moves west to east, rain could be heading my way. A rainbow in the afternoon would mean it appears in the east, so the rain clouds have likely passed me by.

Rainbows were seen by many cultures as bridges or paths to the realm of the gods. Ideas differ on whether or not it is lucky to point at a rainbow; in some beliefs it is, while others say it offends and angers the gods. In some parts of Europe, there is lore that walking under a rainbow is very unlucky, since the rain that falls from it is "blighted." Now that you understand how they form, I think we can all rest easy that we are safe from that one.

It seems there is a split on whether rainbows are lucky or unlucky. I choose to see them as lucky. Your mileage may vary. Maybe just appreciate them for their beauty.

Frogs croak loudly before rain.

They also croak loudly after it passes by! My grandpa always said they were "hollerin', 'Water, more water.'" This is somewhat true; frogs need a freshwater body to lay their eggs in, so if a good rain is on the way, it means breeding will be more successful. The male frogs are hoping to sing up a storm, so to speak, to woo their ladyloves.

When cattle lie down, it means it is about to rain
and sheep huddle up before rain or snow.

These sayings may have some merit, since animals can be sensitive to pressure changes that precede precipitation. These sayings both stem from the idea that the animals want to conserve body heat in case of cold rain or snow.

WINDING IT UP

I will say again, all magic is local. I enjoy supporting my friends who are magical toolmakers, and often do so to the detriment of my bank account. However, I also use what Mother Nature provides as much as possible in my magical work. It deepens my connection to her and to my land. Understanding the science of rain gives me more layers to those connections.

I encourage you to explore working with rain as a magical ally. It would be simple to start out collecting rainwater for your magical use. Pay attention to how that work feels different from using other types of water. Then explore other ways you can use rain in your practice. Follow your intuition and instinct and you will find the right way for you! Water is a powerful magical tool, so why not use what Mother Nature provides us? You may also discover it deepens your connection to her!

Chapter 7

SNOW AND OTHER WINTER WEATHER

As I am writing this, the remnants of the first snowfall here in the Ozarks is melting away. It came very early this year and as a bit of a surprise, but it never fails to make me feel peaceful to see the world blanketed in white. But too much snow causes us Southerners to go into full panic "fights at the grocery store over the last loaf of bread" mode. Snow actually does not worry me as much as its nastier cousin, freezing rain.

Snow also has a rich hidden store of magical potential. It hides the treasures of sacred geometry and numerology within it. It also carries all the energy tied to the phase changes the water vapor has to go through. Understanding how winter weather happens gives me even more opportunities to tap into its energy for magical purposes.

WINTER PRECIPITATION

Snow is probably the most commonly known winter precipitation but is the least well understood by most people. Snow is actually the starting point for most precipitation that reaches the ground. Even in summer, the upper parts of the clouds are cold enough that the precipitation is snow, but it melts as it moves lower in the cloud.

You can actually find the cloud's freezing level if the sun is shining near a cloud on the horizon where precipitation is falling. Snow is much more efficient at scattering sunlight than liquid water, so the falling snow will cause the area below the cloud to look darker than if it were simply raining. You can clearly see that freezing level! You can even see snow falling from high cirrus clouds. If you have ever noticed what looks like streamers coming from those cirrus clouds, those are fallstreaks—ice crystals or snowflakes coming from those clouds. The drier air at that altitude means those fallstreaks dissipate quickly, similar to how virga evaporates at lower altitudes. Fallstreaks from cirrus clouds can happen at any time of the year but can occasionally happen at lower levels during colder parts of the year.

What we think of as snowflakes are actually dendrites, but winter precipitation comes in a variety of forms. In fact, not all snow is the familiar snowflake shape we cut out of paper for winter decorations. Those beautiful, fragile beauties form in very specific conditions. To really understand how the different shapes form, first let's get a handle on the idea of supersaturation.

Supersaturation

Supersaturation happens when there is more water vapor in the air than the air can hold at that temperature. Condensation can't occur easily since there is a lack of those pesky condensation nuclei. A great related example of supersaturation is when you are making fudge.

Figure 9: Snowflake Shapes

Have you ever had a batch of fudge form a layer of sugar crystals over it as it cools down? This is because fudge contains more sugar in the solution than it should be able to hold at room temperature. Anything that can create a condensation nucleus or disturb the cooling process can cause larger crystals of sugar to grow and your fudge will be grainy from the sugar. So at critical times in the process, you have to handle the fudge with care. For example, when making the syrup, you stop stirring when the syrup boils because at this point the crystals have all dissolved and the agitation of stirring can cause crystals to form. There are other rules, too, and reading them, it definitely sounds like fudge making is an act of magic on par with getting your divinity to set, but that is a conversation for another time.

In the cloud, the supersaturated water is looking for those tiny specks of dust that will be the condensation points for all those water molecules. That is the start of our snowflake!

Inside the Snowflake

The next bit of magical beauty, the shape, comes from the atoms that make up the water. Two hydrogen atoms and one oxygen atom arrange themselves in a shape that is often described as a "mouse hat" from that famous mouse place with castles and such.

The bonding of the water molecules as they collect is what is known as hydrogen bonding. Hydrogen bonding is the unique reason water is so "sticky," that is, adheres to itself so well. It is why droplets of water are those near-perfect spheres once they form and also why snowflakes have hexagonal shapes. So much juicy magical geometry and numerology hiding inside that hydrogen bond!

You might be surprised to learn that the familiar hexagonal flake is more complex in variety than you think. For example, some come in the form of simple hexagonal plates, without the radiating arms. These simple prisms can be flat thin plates, or they can grow into columns or needlelike shapes. There is a delicate balance of temperature in the cloud, in the supersaturation level, and in how much time the flakes have to collect water and let it freeze before they fall out of the clouds.

Magic in a Snowflake

Inside the snowflake, there are wonderful opportunities to boost your energy work. First, go back to the snowflake structure. The angle between the hydrogen atoms is 104.5 degrees. So, if I add up all the digits then reduce the total (ten) to a single number, it's a one. If I take the atomic number of oxygen (eight) and the atomic number of hydrogen (one) and add up the number of all the atoms, again it's a one (eight plus one plus one).

Using numerology, some properties associated with the number one are the following:[27]

- positive: intelligent, courageous, inventive, creative, positive
- negative: cold, unfeeling, stubborn, selfish, tactless

Another area to explore is sacred geometry. The hexagon is the unit structure of snowflakes and ice crystals. It is a powerful shape that shows up frequently in nature, and it's a foundational piece to shapes like the Flower of Life. The Flower of Life is a powerful fundamental shape in sacred geometry that shows the interconnectedness of all things.[28]

27.   Bauer, *Numerology for Beginners*, 25.

28.   Brewer, *Sacred Geometry Book of History*, 71.

CRAFT
Snowflake Magic Oracle Cards

Another approach to snowflake magic is thinking about the way they grow, branching, reaching out, responding to changes in their environment.[29] The shape depends on a delicate balance of the temperature and saturation. So, snowflakes require perfect timing. The following project incorporates numerology, sacred geometry, and shape.

You will need
- snowflake images
- cardstock or other heavy paper
- a writing instrument

Directions
You can make these cards anytime. Print out, sketch, or paint images of the snowflakes you have chosen on the cardstock. On the reverse side, write the meanings you want to assign to each snowflake shape. Incorporate the ideas from this chapter about sacred geometry, numerology, science, and lore to give your cards interpretations that have meaning to you. Use the deck as you would any oracle deck.

WINTERY MIX

Graupel forms when snowflakes fall from high in a cloud through a region that has supercooled water. This water collects onto the flake. It freezes to form a soft opaque coating. This softness and the difference in the way it forms distinguishes it from sleet or

---

29. Libbrecht, *Art of the Snowflake*, 11.

hail. When it falls, it looks like those Styrofoam pellets used for packing.

Sleet forms when the snowflake that forms higher in the cloud falls through a warmer layer, causing it to melt into a raindrop. Then this raindrop falls through another freezing layer that is thick enough to cause the drop to refreeze into an ice pellet.

Freezing rain is a familiar nemesis here in the Ozarks. Every few years we get a whopper of an ice storm that brings down trees, powerlines, and the occasional structure. Any person who has gone without power for days or even weeks due to an ice storm knows that this ice accumulation can be heavy! Or it can form a layer of black ice on the roadway, causing driving to become more of an adventure than many of us want.

Freezing rain forms when the second freezing layer isn't thick enough to completely refreeze the raindrop, so it falls as supercooled water. Once it hits the cold surfaces at ground level, it basically flash freezes. This leaves an ice coating on all these objects, and before long, enough has accumulated to break the branches. It only takes a quarter of an inch of this ice layer to start bringing down utility lines!

Ice storms can cause significant damage to trees and leave people without electricity for long periods of time due to substantial damage to power lines. The ice storm of 2009 here in the Ozarks left some small communities without power for nearly a month.

Freezing drizzle and freezing fog can often catch people by surprise since it can create hazardous conditions on roads and bridges. It can also form rime—accumulation of white granular ice on objects over time as the fog or drizzle persists. This can build up in the same way that the ice from freezing rain does, causing similar problems. It is also the phenomenon that causes cloud droplets to freeze on airplanes, causing icing on the wings.

EXERCISE
Icicle Spell

The original inspiration for this work was Dorothy Morrison's Swifting Ritual.[30] Instead of using candles, I use icicles. You can inscribe words or symbols into the icicle and let it melt away. The natural shape of an icicle as a pointer lends itself to work similar to that of the original ritual.

You will need
- an icicle
- salt
- a tray to collect the melted water
- 2 pieces of paper
- a writing instrument

Directions
In the tray, pour a salt arrow long enough to lay the icicle over it. On one piece of paper, write the situation that is currently the one you wish to affect. On the other piece of paper, write your desired evolution of the situation.

Place the first paper at the back end of the arrow of salt. Place the second paper at the pointy end of the arrow of salt. Lay the icicle so that the pointy end lines up with the pointy end of the salt arrow.

---

30. Morrison, *Utterly Wicked*, 102–104.

Stand at the back end of your arrow and visualize the energy of the melting icicle flowing into the work and running toward the desired outcome. If you wish, you can even hold your hands in front of you and move them as though you are pushing the energy out of the pointy tip of the arrow and into the paper with your desired outcome.

When you feel you are ready, simply leave the icicle in place and let it finish melting. Once it has completely melted, pour the water down the sink. Don't pour it on a plant since the salt will not be good for it! Allow your papers to dry out, then burn them to release that energy back into the universe.

I layer the icicle over my line of salt. The clarity of the ice helps my clear seeing of the change, the melting of the ice is the warming up of the situation, and the water allows me to emotionally process the change. I can even collect melted water from the ice or snow and keep it for "cooling" work.

Winter Weather Timing

I often hear people bemoaning how the weather forecasts for winter weather are off the mark. The fact is, winter weather is difficult because it is so sensitive to timing and conditions. Surely as energy workers and magic practitioners, we can relate to this! What type of precipitation falls is dependent on the temperature profile in the cloud. For example, if the entire vertical temperature profile of the cloud stays below freezing, snow of some form will fall. If the profile starts out with freezing at higher altitudes then has a warmer layer followed by another freezing layer, the precipitation will be sleet or freezing rain.

A phrase that has captured many people's attention the past several years is *polar vortex*. We hear these vortices spoken about in the news and on weather stations as if they are some remarkable new phenomena when, in reality, they have always been part of our weather landscape. A polar vortex is simply a large area of low pressure and cold air that surrounds both the polar regions. This system has always been with us. It's just that we seem to be paying more attention to it, particularly now that there is a notable effect of climate change on these phenomena.

Remember that low-pressure systems rotate counterclockwise in the northern hemisphere, clockwise in the southern hemisphere. The strength of these low-pressure systems varies seasonally, being stronger in the winter and weaker in the summer. In the winter, they can cycle through periods of strengthening and weakening. As they weaken, they often have outbreaks where they send cold air southward along the jet stream (I'll stick to the northern hemisphere for the purposes of my description).

The polar vortex is not a surface phenomenon. The base of the polar vortex begins in the middle to upper troposphere and extends into the stratosphere. Underneath this vortex is a mass of cold, dry arctic air. Where it meets the warmer, more humid air to the south defines the polar front. As the vortex cycles, it can push this cold air southward, causing extreme winter weather across much of North America. The jets are pushed farther north, but when outbreaks do occur, the associated weather becomes more extreme.

EXERCISE
Cool It Off Spell

I use temperature drops to my advantage when I need to "cool off" a situation or slow something down. I can pay attention to the temperature change even overnight and determine a way to time my energy work. The past few days here, we had an extremely cold weather system move through, so if something really needed to be stopped in its magical tracks, that gives me a perfect opportunity.

You will need
- a cold weather forecast
- a shallow pan of water
- a location to place the pan of water
- slips of paper and a writing instrument

Directions
Timing of this work should be when below-freezing weather is forecasted.

On the slips of paper, write things that pertain to the situation you want to cool off or freeze out. Place the slips in the water. As you place your slips of paper, focus on the situations you want to affect by this work. Repeat the following three times after you place the slips:

Winter's chill
Heed my will
Slow the pace
Or freeze in place
Let the cold

Put things on hold
Until I say
The warm-up day

Leave the tray in a safe location to let it freeze from the cold air. If you want to keep these things on ice, as it were, move the tray into the freezer or take the ice, put it in a freezer bag, and set it in the freezer.

Exercise extension

An extension of this is to reverse the process to allow a situation to warm up and thaw out gradually as the temperature outside warms. Another option is to take the pieces of ice and place them around plants so as they melt the energy and intention melt into the soil and nourish the soil and the plant.

Even if you live in a more tropical area, watch the temperature changes. To me, my most powerful magic is when I remember "all magic is local," at least the source of the energy I draw from. I do my best work when I tap into that energy closest to me that I interact with daily. "Freezing something out" may mean you use the cooler temps where you are even if they aren't below freezing. The energy is still there, and you can use it to manifest the change you wish to see.

WINTER STORMS

Winter storms come in a range of severity. Snow flurries are usually light amounts of snowfall that tend to fall from cumuliform clouds. A snow squall is a brief but intense snowfall similar to an afternoon summertime thunderstorm. Sometimes the conditions can be right for a cumulonimbus cloud to produce snow. It will still have all the conditions for lightning and thunder, so in that case, it is a rare thundersnow event. Snowfall from cumulus-type clouds is usually brief in duration without significant accumulation.

Longer-period snowfalls occur from stratiform clouds such as nimbostratus or in some cases altostratus clouds. These weather systems can have snowfall that lasts for hours, causing significant accumulations in the affected areas. A blizzard occurs when conditions create dry fine snow particles that are blown by winds, creating poor visibility. These conditions have to last for at least three hours to be considered a blizzard.

ACTIVITY
Snow Day!

As a farmer, I have to pay very close attention to the winter weather forecast. I need to plan for it to be at least as bad as the forecast predicts to make sure my cattle and horses have what they need to survive. As a university professor, I still respect the sanctity of the snow day and enjoy the quiet beauty a rare snowfall brings to the farm.

Let's say there is a change of snow in the forecast, and like when I was a kid, I want a snow day. I will make my own snowstorm in hopes of enticing the snowfall so I get my snow day. You can try it too!

You will need
- paper
- scissors

Directions

Do this work whenever you want to have fun making snowflakes, but if you want a snow day, check the forecast for snow heading your way!

You are going to make the snowflakes like you might have done in grade school, but now adding intention. Begin by folding your paper diagonally so that the top edge lines up with one of the side edges. Trim away excess so that you are left with a square of paper if you open the diagonal fold.

Fold back along the diagonal as the paper was when you trimmed. Fold in half again. Fold this triangle into thirds so you will have six sectors for your snowflake. Flatten the top edge by cutting off the points.

You can proceed two ways. One is just to cut designs in the paper and unfold it and be surprised. The other is to find a template or create one and trace it onto your sector, then cut it out. While you are cutting out your snowflake, focus on your intention of a snow day. Recite this verse as you cut out your snowflake:

> *Snow day, snow day, come my way*
> *Let the snow come so I can play*
> *Snow day, snow day, happen soon*
> *May the snow clouds grant this boon!*

Cut out as many snowflakes as you wish and hang them up. Then wait to get the message that your snow day wish has been granted!

WINTER WEATHER OPTICAL PHENOMENA

There are some atmospheric optical phenomena that are caused by ice in the atmosphere. The "ring around the moon" we talked about in the clouds chapter is one of those. What we see depends on which surface of the hexagonal ice crystal the sunlight hits. Parhelia, or sundogs, occur for similar reasons as the rings around the sun or moon but the light is hitting thinner, plate-shaped ice crystals instead of the longer cylindrical ice crystals that make the halos. Sundogs are bright, slightly elongated streaks of light on either side of the sun. They look like chunks of the halo shape, but the rest of the halo is missing. They can have rainbow colors, or they can look like small suns. This is why they are sometimes called mock suns.

Another ice-related atmospheric phenomenon is a sun pillar. Sun pillars are seen at sunrise or sunset. They appear as a faint column of light above the point where the sun is below the horizon. These also need the plate-shaped crystals that make the sundogs, but many more, and they need to be closer to the ground. Sadly, many of us who live in more temperate climates don't get a chance to see these often, since it is hard for the ice crystals to persist that low in the atmosphere. Very bright outdoor lights can cause the same effect.

More Magical Inspiration

There are so many things about snow that could be folded into my practice. When I walk outside after a snowfall, only the sounds nearest me are easily heard; the rest are muffled by the softness of the snow. This is a good time for me to sit in silence and listen for the messages only meant for me, those nearest and dearest to me. The noise and static of all the other things surrounding me are quieted. It is time for Spirit to communicate directly and clearly with me.

Snow is a good thermal insulator, keeping heat in, so I have used snow as a component in a protection spell. I will write my intent, or the person's name, and prepare a spell jar I will then bury in the snow. I use this for more temporary protection work, like safe traveling or for a medical procedure, since the snow will eventually melt.

We rarely get large accumulations of snow here, but when we do, I like to catch it in buckets or bowls. I will bring it inside and let it melt and save the water for use in my practice. The snowmelt, to me, still contains all the energy of the formation and structure of the snowflake (we'll talk about this more in a bit).

The snowmelt water seems to me extra clear and fresh, so I use it to bless or cleanse my tools or altar pieces. It's perfect for dressing a candle to add that extra snow energy to your work. Remember all the things we just said about it softening, insulating, or cleaning the slate. I will use those ideas in my intention when I am adding snowmelt to my candle.

If I happen to get enough to use in my scrying or healing bowl, I will save it in a special jar until I need it. A good rule of thumb is it is a ten-to-one ratio for snow to melted water. It takes ten inches of snowfall to equal one inch of water. I don't get to do this very often here, but maybe you can.

Because snow and ice are liquid water that has undergone a transformation, using them for working toward change or transformation would be appropriate. I have a half-gallon jar of snowmelt water I use for dressing candles and my altar bowls. You could use the water from snow or ice to "write" spells or intention out, or even to mix up a dye or ink.

WINTER WEATHER LORE

As a farmer, it is no surprise to me that winter weather merits its own lore. Winter weather can have a devastating impact on crops and livestock, so being forewarned of coming storms is exceedingly valuable. However, being weather wise about winter storms isn't just valuable to farmers; everyone can use this knowledge since it can impact travel plans, grocery shopping, utilities, and even emergency services. Let's get prepared.

> *When the snow falls dry, it means to lie.*
> *But flakes light and soft bring rain oft.*

Dry snow usually forms at lower temperatures, so when it falls, the colder temperatures mean it will stick around a while. The larger, fluffier flakes are created with warmer temperatures, so often the profile will switch from snow to rain due to the warmer air.

The same rationale is the science behind the saying "when snow melts off the roof, the next storm will be rain. When the snow blows off, reckon on snow."

> *Bearded frost, forerunner of snow.*

The bearded frost is a type of ice that forms on dead wood or other vegetation, and it takes on the shape of fine hair. It forms when the temperatures are slightly less than freezing and the air is humid. This combination can often herald snow.

> *If it snows fine and small, one can expect great, persistent cold;*
> *if it snows with large and broad flakes, moderate cold.*

This German saying is actually accurate. The colder the air, the dryer, so larger flakes don't form. The ones that do are the finer, smaller shapes of crystals.

Snow never leaves ice behind.

This Italian saying has a couple of potential meanings. One could be that often snow will sublimate instead of melt, going directly from a solid to water vapor. Alternately, it could mean that it takes more time for the snow to melt, so any accompanying ice is long gone by the time it does.

Unfortunately, many of the lore sayings about the amount of snow that comes in winter being related to sunny days or foggy days in the summer has no real scientific basis. There is one that does have some truth to it, however: "As the days lengthen, the cold strengthens." This happens to be valid, since even though the winter solstice is the shortest day, the coldest months lag behind due to that specific heat phenomenon we talked about earlier. The months following the solstice tend to be the colder months of winter just as the months following the summer solstice tend to be hotter for the same reason.

Just because the sayings like "for every fog in August, there will be a snowfall in winter" don't seem to have any scientific backing, it's still fun to keep track of those things and see for yourself. I keep a little datebook or almanac at the ready and try to record things in it for each day.

Also, even though I know there isn't at present a scientific reason for it, I still gather a ripe persimmon in the fall and cut the seed open to look at the shape inside. The shapes are supposed to remind you of a knife, fork, or spoon, and the shape you see indicates the severity of the coming winter. Spoons mean heavy snow, knives mean especially cold cutting winds and temperatures, while forks mean it will be mild. There is even an Ag Extension office in Missouri that has collected this data for a couple of decades, and according to them, it's about 75 percent accurate.

Woolly bear caterpillars, the larval stage of the Isabella moth, are another winter weather predictor. They have bands of black and rust coloring on their bodies. According to the lore, the more black a caterpillar has on it, the more severe the coming winter. Some people look at the activity of squirrels or their horses' coats. There are lots of animal-related pieces of lore about weather, so we will explore those also, because as a farmer how can I not?

Some of the other prognosticators for winter weather include the following: "When pigs gather leaves and straw in the fall, expect a cold winter"; "When rabbits are fat in the fall, expect a long, cold winter"; and my personal favorite, "If the mole digs its hole two and a half feet deep, expect severe weather; if two feet deep, not so severe; if one foot deep, a mild winter." I'm pretty sure the moles would be annoyed if we excavated their holes for measuring purposes.

WINDING IT UP

Winter weather can be both beautiful and troublesome. It is rich in energy, so it's full of potential for magical work. That energy is hidden inside the phase changes that take the water vapor into its solid forms of ice or snowflakes. It is hidden inside the geometry of the snowflake. It is hidden inside the shape of an icicle.

As a scientist, I marvel at all the science embedded in a winter snowstorm, how a small change in timing makes a big difference in the amount of snowfall I get or how a seemingly small amount of freezing rain can cause a mighty tree to snap. As a farmer, I have a healthy respect for winter weather since I am responsible for the well-being of my animals, plus living in a rural area, I need to be prepared for possibly prolonged power outages. As a witch, it seems a natural next step to tap into all the energy and potential a snowstorm has for my magical practice.

The next time you are wishing for a snow day, I hope you spend some time thinking about the structure of those snow-flakes. Pause for a minute and think of all the richness of the patterns inside them. Then, think about all the processes that it took to make that snowflake and all the energy involved. I hope you will explore what you have learned and add those ideas to your magical practice and make them your own.

Chapter 8

THUNDERSTORMS
Big Energy, Big Magic

Living where I do, in the foothills of the Arkansas Ozarks, I am well familiar with thunderstorms, both the predictable summer afternoon variety and the more ominous supercell variety. The science of what allows them to form is very similar, but the actual conditions they form under are very different. Both types need updraft—the rising of warm, humid air—as their energy source. That energy is the same powerful storehouse I draw from in my magical practice.

AFTERNOON THUNDERSTORMS

The summer afternoon storms are familiar to many of us; in fact, some people swear you could set your clock by them in certain places. These storms rely on the localized convection of the afternoon heating to form. Remember the chapter on cloud formation? Storms occur when the afternoon heating allows those towering cumulonimbus clouds to form.

I have spent many an afternoon in the hayfield watching these storms form. When we would head out to work hay in the morning, the sky would be perfectly clear. The morning would move along in the lazy way that time spins out in the summer, the temperature and humidity rising. Once we would break for dinner (or lunch for the non-hayfield folk in the crowd), we would notice a few small puffy cumulus clouds in the sky.

Building Phase

During the building phase, those clouds have started building up, maybe looking a little less friendly and a lot stormier. The buildup was caused by the rising of the warm air from the surface. Since it was a typical Arkansas summer afternoon, the humidity felt somewhere between being inside a sauna and being in a tropical rainforest. It was this key ingredient that would mean soon we could very well have a thunderstorm.

In the summer weather forecasts here, there will be a perpetual 20 percent chance of storms and the weatherperson calling for scattered showers. The scattered shower prediction comes from not knowing exactly where these storms will fire up. I might get rain, but probably not. These are the kinds of storms where it is raining across the road from my house but not *at* my house.

If I am so inclined, and I often am, I can sit in my lawn chair and watch one of these storms go through their entire life cycle. Talk about some juicy goodness for spell timing. These storms are sometimes called air mass or ordinary cell thunderstorms. They are tied to the heating of the earth and water by the sun, causing the air to warm and rise. All four elements work in balance to create these storms, so they are rich sources of energy for spell work.

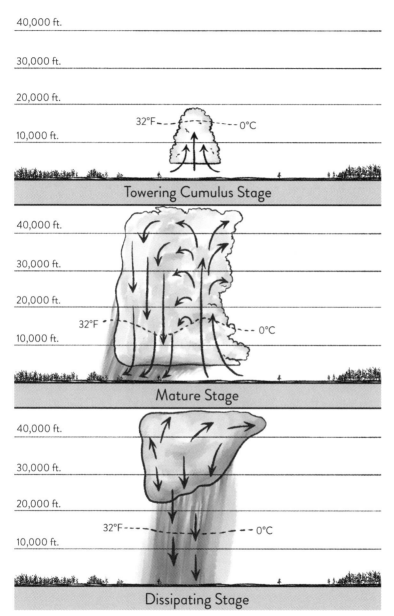

Figure 10: Convective Thunderstorm Life Cycle

The heated air parcel rises just like I described in the clouds chapter. Except this time, they rise to the point that condensation starts to form raindrops or, at high enough altitudes, ice particles. As the updraft from the heating continues, there is a source of more humid air and energy for the storm to build. This is the towering cumulus phase we see as the little cumulus clouds start to look more foreboding. As the updraft continues, the particles will be prevented from falling, so they grow to a larger size. The cloud eventually builds up to the familiar cumulonimbus anvil.

Mature Phase

The raindrops or ice particles will eventually grow to a size that the updraft can no longer hold them suspended. As they fall, their friction with the air molecules around them causes a downdraft to form. Eventually, they will fall out of the cloud as rain, the ice having melted as it passes through the lower, warmer layers of the cloud. Where the rain exits the bottom layer is called the rain shaft. The base of the cloud looks like someone punched a hole in it with granny's biscuit cutter. That's the location of the rain shaft and where the downdraft is exiting the cloud.

It also heralds the beginning of the end of the little afternoon thunderstorm. The downdraft is now blocking part of the updraft and thus preventing some energy from getting into the storm. This causes the updraft to weaken and allows the downdraft to get strong, letting the rain shaft grow.

If I am in my lawn chair watching, I will notice the hole in the base of the cloud starting to grow in diameter. More rain will begin falling out of the base of the cloud, and it could even have some lightning and small hail.

ACTIVITY
Collecting Thunderstorm Water

Thunderstorm water is a powerful addition to your magical tool kit. I use thunderstorm water in all the ways I would use regular water in my work. If you work with a storm deity, it is the perfect water to use for offerings or to bless statues, candles, or tools dedicated to that practice. If I am making a healing bowl, I will add some thunderstorm water to give an extra boost to the energy I am sending.

You will need
- a bowl or other collection container
- safe location to place container
- stones to hold container down (if needed)

Directions
Prepare your container by cleansing it ahead of time. Sit your bowl out ahead of the storm's arrival.

Once the water has been collected, strain it to remove any plant matter that may have blown in and store.

Exercise extension
Another way I collect thunderstorm water is to look for it collected in rock hollows while I am hiking. I will carry an empty water bottle for such a purpose. If I happen across a small pool of stormwater that has collected in a rock cavity, I will gather some up (of course asking permission of the land spirits to do so). I only take a little bit, leaving most of it behind out of courtesy. Now the water has the energy of the storm as well as the earth.

EXERCISE
Thunderstorm Water Scrying

Often, as the thunderstorms pass through, there is clearing weather and the air feels refreshed and clean. Taking this same idea into scrying, imagine that the thunderstorm water will give you a clearer or fresher perspective on what you are focusing on.

You will need
- thunderstorm water
- a scrying bowl
- clear quartz (optional)

Directions

Prepare yourself and your space. There are many ways to do this, but I use the method similar to the way described by Diana Palm.[31]

Pour your thunderstorm water in the bowl. If it helps your focus, add a piece of clear quartz since it enhances psychic ability.[32] Settle in a comfortable position with the bowl within arm's reach. Take a few deep breaths to center and focus.

Relax your gaze as you look at the surface of the water. Try to focus on the crystal. Gently blow across the surface of the water. Note any shapes or images you see on the water's surface.

Once you are done with your scrying session, be sure to disengage any energetic connections you created to scry.

31. Palm, *Mediumship Scrying & Transfiguration for Beginners*, 50.
32. Hall, *Crystal Bible*, 225.

Take a few deep breaths to once again ground and center yourself and to restore your balance after the session.

After using the water for your session, pour it out on the earth, allowing its energy to be recycled by the water cycle for future use.

DISSIPATION PHASE

These little afternoon thunderstorms do occasionally get strong enough to be ranked as "severe." The National Weather Service defines a severe thunderstorm as one that produces one-inch or larger hail or has wind speeds of greater than fifty-eight miles per hour. These afternoon storms do occasionally produce small, weak tornados. Tornados will be discussed more in a later chapter.

As the downdraft takes over the cloud, the updraft is effectively blocked, and now the storm lacks an energy source. As I watch the cloud, I notice it has started to "rain itself out," meaning you can literally watch the cloud disappear from the bottom up. As the energy and water vapor are expended, the cloud dissipates, often just leaving behind the anvil tops. These "orphaned anvils" are all that remain of the afternoon storm.

Because of the way they are formed, these storms generally don't travel much. That is why I can have rain close enough that I can smell it or even see it, but no rain will fall at my location. That doesn't mean, however, that the storms aren't of concern, especially if they are producing lightning.

These storms do often create a chain reaction in the afternoon. As one storm's downdraft starts to build, it can force nearby air parcels upward, effectively pushing them out of the way. Once this updraft is triggered, a new storm begins to build. As the second storm matures and its downdraft grows, it can trigger the formation of yet another storm near it. So, a lot like popcorn, these storms continue to pop up all afternoon. If I am still out there in my lawn chair watching, I get to see this train of storms in their various stages of development. That is one of my favorite things to look for if I can't benefit from the much-needed rain that is happening across the way!

Once the sun sets, the show is over. The sun was the source of that heating, and once it's below the horizon, there isn't enough energy to produce any more updrafts. So the last of the storms rain themselves out and things quiet down for the night. Then the next day, if the right conditions exist, it all starts again!

EXERCISE
Afternoon Storms, Afternoon Magic

As an energy worker and a magic practitioner, to me, it makes sense to use the predictability of these afternoon thunderstorms as a source of energy in my magical practice. I know that in the summer here in the Ozarks, many days I will get afternoon "heating" thunderstorms. Around lunch, the morning's clear sky will become host to those puffy cumulus clouds (technically cumulus humilis), then around midafternoon, the clouds begin to boil up as the sun heats the atmosphere. Before long, I will hear thunder in the distance.

Maybe I have some spell work that would benefit from a little extra boost of energy. Timing my spell work to match the development of the storms in the afternoon makes sense.

You will need

- a comfortable location to view the thunderstorm developing
- water-soluble nontoxic ink or paint
- a writing instrument or paintbrush
- paper

Directions

Timing this during the emerging storm will benefit something you wish to grow or develop. If you instead want to release, time this for the dissipation phase of the storm.

The storm doesn't need to be at your location. You can watch a storm in the distance and practice this work just as easily. Remember, these afternoon heating thunderstorms are called scattered for a reason. They may very well not form where you are, but that energy is still in the atmosphere for us to access.

Settle in your comfortable location, and when you see the storm at the right development phase, begin your work.

Write or draw something on the paper that represents your intention using the water-soluble medium you chose. I particularly like to use those inexpensive watercolors we all got back in grade school since they are easy to find!

As you are working on your paper, visualize the energy in the storm streaming from it and into your paper, fueling your intent. Continue adding to your paper as long as you feel it is necessary for your work to be complete or when the life cycle of the storm you are using has ended.

If the storm is near enough to rain at your location, if you wish, leave your paper where the rain can wash the ink off to add the extra boost of rainfall's magic to your work. If not, take the paper with you as a reminder of the work you set in motion.

Thank the storm for adding its energy to your work. If you can't make it outside during the thunderstorm, you can still do this work indoors.

EXERCISE
Drawing Rain

When I am needing rain, I try to encourage these pop-up storms to come my way. As a farmer and gardener, rain at the right time is critical for a successful year.

You will need
- a bowl of water (if you have rainwater or thunderstorm water, use that)
- a tree branch (try to use a branch from a tree that grows near water)

Directions
I will usually use a bowl of water and a willow branch from my creek. If I have a special bowl in my magical tools, I can use that. However, as my family would admonish, "Use what you got!" so I have not been above using a wooden spoon and a mixing bowl. My rule is to use whatever I have at hand when the need strikes.

Time this work when the afternoon convective thunderstorms are beginning to form in your area.

Fill the bowl about halfway with water. Begin to stir the water counterclockwise. (I know this is widdershins, but remember that you are trying to create a low-pressure system to draw the rain to your location. Low pressure rotates counterclockwise in the northern hemisphere.)

As you stir, recite these words three times:

> *Rain, rain, come to me*
> *I call upon your energy*
> *Rain, rain, drench the earth*
> *End this water dearth*
> *Rain, rain, come this way*
> *Quench the land on this day*

After reciting the verse three times, set the bowl down and place the tree branch across it. Wait for the rain to come! When it does, be sure to thank it for quenching the land's thirst.

Exercise extension

If instead you want the rain to go away, try this. Instead of stirring counterclockwise, stir clockwise. Alter the verse to ask the storm to pass you by. If you don't have a way to get a branch and a bowl of water, just use a clockwise hand motion.

STRONGER THUNDERSTORMS

The other types of thunderstorms are the multicell storms, squall line storms, and supercell storms. Multicell storms are stronger than the single-cell storms, containing multiple storms at various stages of development, but their updraft comes from a vertical wind shear often caused by a gust front. A gust front is when a strong, cold downdraft reaches the surface and spreads out, pushing underneath the warm moist surface air, forcing it aloft. The storms are pushed along by horizontal winds aloft, but the gust front can spread out in multiple directions, stimulating new cell development, especially in front of the storm.

These gust fronts sometimes cause the formation of a shelf cloud in front of the storm that can look rather ominous, but it is still the leading edge of the wind shear. Sometimes, a roll cloud will form from similar conditions, except the roll cloud completely detaches itself from the base of the thunderstorm and "tumbles along" under the leading edge. It rolls in a horizontal fashion, sometimes freaking people out because they think it is a tornado. Fortunately, roll clouds only *look* scary.

On the other hand, a particularly strong thunderstorm can create a dangerous condition called a downburst. The downburst happens with storms that have strong updrafts. Remember, the updraft is what holds the rain or sometimes hail suspended in the cloud. So long as the updraft stays strong enough to hold it, this core of rain or hail will stay put. The problem occurs when something causes the updraft to weaken, such as cooling due to evaporation or rainfall from another nearby cell. If the updraft weakens, it can't hold this large core buildup and it comes rapidly crashing toward the ground.

The wind speeds in these downbursts, or their smaller but just as dangerous sibling the microburst, can exceed one hundred miles per hour. This can spell disaster for structures, planes, or really anything that happens to be in the vicinity of this downburst. Fortunately, weather forecasters can now recognize the conditions in a thunderstorm that can lead to a microburst, so it makes plane travel much safer. Remember that the next time your flight gets diverted because of a thunderstorm! It's not about being an inconvenience; it really is about keeping people safe.

Squall Line Thunderstorms

Squall line thunderstorms are common in my part of the world, both in the spring and in the fall when the atmosphere is shifting gears from winter to summer or vice versa. Squall lines are fast-moving storms that line up along the frontal boundary of a cold front. So long as the cold front is intercepting the warm moist air ahead of it, these storms will have an energy source. These storms can occur at any time, day or night, but can be stronger than usual if they benefit from afternoon heating from the sun in addition to the energy from the front.

These storms blow through along this boundary and may only be dozens of miles wide, but the line itself can be hundreds of lines long. Here in the United States, the line can span several states. These storms can produce tornados, but not as readily as their supercell kin, nor will the tornados be as strong as the ones from supercells. One reason is the line of storms is essentially competing for energy, and so no single storm can gobble up the lion's share of that energy from the specific heat capacity of water.

The gust front from the squall line can sometimes cause another squall line to form in front of the one along the frontal boundary. This prefrontal line of storms can actually cool off the air before the squall line arrives and maybe lessen the strength of the main storms. I am always happy to see those smaller, weaker storms come in first because I know they are likely providing some mitigation to the storms that come along later.

Derechos

Although squall line storms are not as likely to form tornados as supercell storms, they can still be quite strong and dangerous. Sometimes the inflow from the cold air pushes in from the rear of the line of storms. These inflow winds can be quite strong and can push the line outward so it appears like it is bowing on the radar image. If the winds are very strong, they can form a large bow echo extending two hundred fifty miles or more with wind speeds in excess of fifty miles per hour. This storm system is called a derecho.

The damage from a derecho can be as extensive as that of a tornado and is often confused for tornado damage. Trust and believe that your insurance adjuster has been schooled to know the difference. The derecho winds are straight line, so the debris will be blown in one direction, unlike the debris from a tornado.

The strong horizontal winds can create a unique occurrence called a gustnado, which is small whirlwinds that form due to eddy currents in the outflow boundary of a strong thunderstorm. What distinguishes gustnados from tornados is they are not connected to the rotating cloud base. They can cause damage but are classified as thunderstorm winds rather than tornadic winds.

At certain times of year, the atmosphere becomes very unstable aloft due to the changing positions and strength of the jet streams. In my part of the world, this is most prevalent during midspring and mid-autumn. This instability can create conditions for the strongest and most dangerous thunderstorms to form. Supercell thunderstorms occur when there is a strong vertical wind shear. This shear can be so strong that the updraft is not snuffed out by the downdraft, so the storms can persist for hours. These supercell storms are the largest of the thunderstorms, as the name implies. A single storm can encompass many miles, and supercells are also the tallest of the thunderstorms. All this adds up to these supercells producing very dangerous weather conditions, including the largest hail and the strongest tornados. We will get into tornados in a later chapter.

HAIL

Living in an area where strong thunderstorms are common, I am painfully familiar with hail. Hailstones can grow to a size where they can become dangerous and destructive, especially in some of the large supercell storms that form over the Great Plains. Hail, especially large hail, is often considered one of the signs that a storm could become tornadic.

Hail forms in a thunderstorm, needing the vertical development of the cumulonimbus cloud to create the updraft the hail needs to form. Hail needs a "seed" to develop around. This can be ice or dust particles, but even the odd unfortunate insect will do. Below the freezing level of the cloud, this seed will begin to accumulate supercooled water droplets. Instead of being able to fall as rain, the strong updraft in the thunderstorm will push it upward above the freezing level. Because this updraft can cause turbulence in the storm, the frozen mass can work its way downward to collect more water droplets. This process may occur multiple times, causing the hailstone to build up in layers of frozen water.

In a strong storm, the updraft may keep this particle aloft long enough to grow to a large size. Most hailstones will at least partially melt as they move through the lower, warmer layers. Some may even completely melt and fall as rain. But if not, look out! Even though it is just past midwinter here, with spring still a couple of months away, after a few very warm days, we had a nasty little thunderstorm last night. I was awakened by the familiar bang and rattle of hail hitting my metal roof. Fortunately it was fairly small hail, but it still was enough to ding up cars, shred vegetation, and cause minor chaos in my yard.

EXERCISE
Hailstone Magic

I have been known to go out after a hailstorm has passed and gather up a few stones to keep in my freezer. I use them in the same way I would ice cubes for magical work, taking advantage of the extra boost of energy the hailstone has gathered from the thunderstorm.

I also like using the concept of the hailstone building up in layers in a visualization to "coat" something in layers of magical work.

You will need
- a comfortable location to sit
- a small pebble

Directions
You could do this visualization anytime, but ideally you could time it when there is a thunderstorm in your area.

Find a comfortable location to settle yourself in. Hold the pebble, which acts as the nucleus of your visualized hailstone. Close your eyes. Take a few deep breaths to ground and center yourself.

Visualize the pebble in your hand moving upward in the thunderstorm, gathering water around it as you go. See the energy of the storm bathing the pebble as the water begins to freeze around it, coating the nucleus in a layer of energetically charged ice. Visualize the pebble moving down, gathering more water. Now see the pebble moving back up and freezing again.

Repeat this until you feel that the energy you need on your hailstone has been built up as much as you want. Visualize the energy filling the nucleus pebble.

When you have finished the energy transfer, feel yourself being grounded back to the earth. Take a few deep breaths to center yourself. Open your eyes. Your nucleus pebble is now ready for whatever energetic work you desire.

You could also gather up actual hailstones (after the storm has passed!) and save those in a freezer to use for magical work.

WEATHER LORE

It makes sense that there is a significant amount of weather lore around thunderstorms. They have always impacted farmers, mariners, hunters, or anyone who makes a living in nature. The awesome power of thunderstorms isn't easily forgotten, so understanding when they were coming was a valuable skill.

The sharper the blast, the sooner 'tis past.

I hope now you see the direct link between that saying and the cold front and squall line storms that would be quite loud and strong but would move through a geographic area quickly.

When the clouds appear like rocks and towers,
the earth's refreshed with frequent showers

or,

> *If in the sky you see cliffs and towers,*
> *it won't be long before there is a shower.*

This bit of lore describes the appearance of cumulonimbus clouds as towers. I think this is especially a good piece of lore to describe the formation of afternoon thunderstorms. It reminds us that the happy little cumulus clouds have to grow and change their appearance for those storms to form.

One saying that is related to the wind shear is "if the clouds move against the wind, rain will follow." If there is a wind shear, the wind at the surface will be blowing a different direction than the winds aloft. This indicates an instability, and storms could very likely form.

> *Hail brings frost on the tail*

or,

> *Hailstorm during the day denotes frost at night.*

Both sayings are tied to the conditions of a cold front forming a thunderstorm. Strong thunderstorms often can form hail, then the temperature would drop as the cold front passes.

> *Under water dearth, under snow bread.*

Heavy rains that cause flooding can destroy crops. A deep snow doesn't have this same effect. A good rule of thumb is every ten inches of snow corresponds to one inch of water. The slow melting of snow will let the water soak in and nourish the soil instead of destroying the crops.

Thunder in spring, cold will bring.

This saying is true in the sense that thunderstorms often form along the frontal boundary of a cold front. Once the storm line passes, the temperatures will drop. In the spring and autumn, this drop can often be significant since the jet streams are still unstable as they move in response to the seasonal changes.

After much thunder, much rain.

Because the sound of thunder can travel a dozen or more miles from the storm, we can often hear thunder from an approaching storm. The thunderstorm will often bring with it hard rains. Another form of this saying is "when it thunders and thunders again, the rain approaches."

Anvil-shaped clouds bring on a gale.

This certainly has some truth to it. The anvil shape of the cumulonimbus clouds means that thunderstorms are in the area. A gale could definitely occur if you happen to have a thunderstorm form near you!

WINDING IT UP

Thunderstorms are part of most places' weather. The energy of their formation comes from the front or the afternoon convection. The energy could also come from the phase changes the water goes through. All that energy is available to you in your practice.

The key here is making it your own! Find what works in your practice. If you don't live in an area where storms are common, when they do occur, that makes them even more special! If there isn't a storm anywhere close, why not draw out a cumulonimbus cloud? Write your intent on the picture, then imagine the balance of energy in the storm feeding your intention. I hope you find a way to use the energy of thunderstorms in your practice.

Chapter 9

LIGHTNING
A Powerful Magical Ally

Even though it is just past midwinter here, we are having an afternoon of strong thunderstorms. I was roused from my sleep by a very close lightning strike. I've had an adversarial relationship with lightning most of my life. It started when I was four or so and my dad had asked me to go get him something out of the refrigerator. There was a huge lightning storm going on outside at the time. About the time I opened the fridge door, lightning hit close enough that it traveled along our metal water line and shot into the sink through the faucet. I just remember a blinding flash and a loud crack. I'm sure I dropped whatever I had in my hands before I bolted from the kitchen. Thus began a lifelong obsession with understanding lightning and learning how to dance with its desire to infiltrate my life at various times. Maybe that was my first step in the journey of becoming both a scientist and a weather witch.

As far as my personal magical work with lightning, I tend to not work with lightning directly due to safety and unpredictability. If I want to view a lightning storm, I do so from a safe location.

I do often put things out in a thunderstorm if I want them magically charged since I consider the lightning energy to be part of the storm as a whole. I will particularly put out any metal objects I use: bowls, blades, bells, anything that can weather the storm (no pun intended) safely.

HOW LIGHTNING FORMS

Lightning at its most basic is nothing more than a massive static spark. Charges separate and build up in the cloud in much the same way we get a buildup of charge on us from scuffing our feet across a carpeted floor. Those charges are essentially marooned on us until we reach for a metal knob. Then the charges that have built up on us cause an induced charge to appear on the knob, and as in life, very often opposites attract, and those charges jump the air gap from us to the knob, creating a small spark.

The mechanism that causes charging in clouds is not as clear, but one of the leading ideas is the clouds become electrically charged from the interaction of the graupel and hail with the supercooled water in the cumulonimbus cloud. Just like when you scuff your feet across the carpet, there is a transfer of charges. In the cloud, the warmer particles come into contact with the colder water; there is a transfer of charges so that the hail or graupel becomes negative and the water becomes positive.

As the heavier, negatively charged objects move downward, there is an accumulation of negative charges in the lower part of the cloud. The upper part of the cloud will be positively charged. This amassing of negative charges causes a positive charge to be induced on the ground below the cloud. Things like trees, buildings, antenna, unaware golfers, and the like could become conduits that connect these charges.

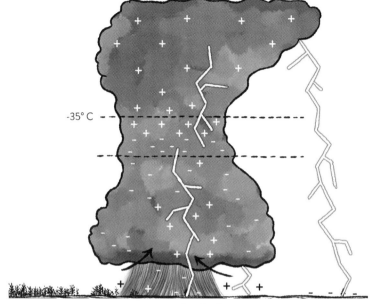

Figure 11: Cloud Charging

Induced Charging

I've mentioned induced charge a couple of times now, so let's talk for a minute about what this actually means. Most things around us are electrically neutral, meaning they have the same number of positive charges and negative charges as part of their makeup. Scuffing my feet across the carpet rips those negative charges off the carpet at the atomic level. That is charging by direct contact because my shoes are pulling the charges off the carpet fibers.

Induced charging is a little bit different. In the case of induction, charges are not removed from or added to anything, meaning the object is still technically electrically neutral. But let's say I bring a charged object near my neutral one. What happens at the atomic level is the like charges will try to get as far away from that object as possible and the opposite charges will be attracted to it. Think about how magnets can push apart from each other, then if you flip one, they will attract each other. This repelling of the charges even though they are still connected in the molecule is called polarization, and it causes neutral things to act like they are electrically charged. Even if there is just a little bit of separation inside the object or even if the molecules become polarized, the effect will still be that the charged object you brought up will attract the neutral one.

Since sometimes it helps to see this for yourself, you can try this at home. If you have a good old-fashioned rubber comb, the kind like my papaw used, comb it through your hair several times. Then take it over to a sink, but be careful you don't let it touch anything. Turn on the tap so a thin stream of water is flowing, then bring the charged comb near the stream. The water will be attracted to the comb and will bend slightly toward it.

Water has two hydrogen atoms and an oxygen atom; because of this, it is very easy for water to polarize. It will react to the comb having all the charges of your hair by polarizing and attracting to the comb. Even though you haven't touched the water, you have still caused it to have an effective charge by inducing the charges to separate. This is similar to what happens to the area under the thunderstorm. The negative charges collecting near the base of the cloud cause the ground underneath to polarize and have an induced positive charge. It's this induced charge that is necessary for lightning to happen.

Lightning Strike

What happens next is a lot like what happens when you have that spark jump between your finger and the doorknob, but with a more dramatic and dangerous effect. As the negative charges continue to build up at the cloud base, some of them begin to "leak" off the cloud to start traveling toward the ground. These leaking charges are called a stepped leader. They are trying to get to the positive patch of ground. This stepped leader makes its way toward the ground, often branching to take multiple paths. This branching happens because the wind is causing the air to shift, so like winding their way through a holiday sale crowd, the negative charges are looking for any clear path to the ground. This initial movement of charges is very faint, so usually invisible to our eye.

These negative charges moving toward the ground attract the positive charges that have been gathering on the ground below the cloud. The upward flow of positive charges, called positive streamers, start working their way up to possibly connect with a stepped leader. Multiple positive streamers may start their way up from the ground. The one that connects will be where the lightning strike occurs. The negative charges flow all the way to the ground, but what we see as the lightning strike is the brighter return stroke, the flow of charges from the ground back up to the cloud. This upward flow is nature's way of trying to balance the electrical charges of the cloud. This is why some people think lightning strikes from the ground up to the cloud because this is the first time it is bright enough to see. This return stroke heats up the gasses in the branched channel, and that is the bright flash called the lightning bolt.

ACTIVITY
Creating a Lightning Protection Amulet

I created a special amulet or charm that I hang on special trees around my farm. My dad once told me we get a lot of lightning strikes up here because of all the iron in the soil. While I've never been able to verify that scientifically, I know our wells always had orange water and the next ridge over is called Iron Ore Mountain. So, I figured better safe than sorry. I came up with this idea using what I know about science but also things I have learned about the magical properties of metals.

Figure 12: Lightning Protection Amulet

You will need
- a copper nail
- an iron nail
- silver 20-gauge beading wire
- quartz crystal point

Directions

Copper is typically used for wiring in houses because it is a good electrical conductor. Copper wires are a way people kill unwanted trees without the use of herbicides. Iron nails are associated with protection.[33] Silver is an excellent conductor of electricity. Quartz is a powerful redirector of energy.[34]

You can make this amulet anytime.

Hold the copper nail so the point is facing downward. Place the iron nail horizontally across the copper nail so it forms a plus sign. Cut a piece of silver wire about eighteen inches long. Holding the wire in the center, wrap the two nails to hold them together. Wrap the upper tail of the wire toward the top of the copper nail, leaving enough length to form a hanging loop at top. Wrap the lower tail of the wire toward the tip of the copper nail, leaving a six- to eight-inch length at the tip of the nail. Use the remaining length to wire wrap the quartz crystal point, making sure the terminated end points toward the ground.

As I am wrapping, I can say a simple protection spell:

---

33.   Weston, *Ozark Mountain Spell Book*, 109.

34.   Melody and P., *Love Is in the Earth*, 503.

To the ground the lightning goes
To the ground the energy flows
To the ground so no harm comes
To the ground protection done

You can hang this anywhere you would like added lightning protection. I hang them on my favorite trees, in my house, and in my barn.

I recently used this charm for our tent at a medieval fair. A late-afternoon thunderstorm popped up in the distance and was a particularly electrically active storm. The public safety officers came over the public address system and announced the storm was headed our way and the fair would shut down until it had passed. I happened to have an amulet in my car. Telling my friends that I would be right back, I ran out to grab it. I returned to our tent and made up a simple protection rhyme that I recited three times. I don't remember the wording exactly (as I have already established, I'm pretty off the cuff in my practice), but it was something like this:

Lightning, lightning, pass by me
There is nothing here for you to see
Lightning, lightning, go away
There is nothing here for you today
Lightning, lightning, do no harm
There is no need for our alarm

I hung the charm on one of the jewelry displays. I positioned it so it was facing the direction of the approaching storm. The storm ended up changing course and headed off to the southwest, so we never had any lightning at our location. I'll happily let my work take a little of the credit for our safety that day.

TYPES OF LIGHTNING

Most of us are familiar with the forked cloud-to-ground lightning. This strike is along a channel like the one described above, with the channel connecting the cloud to the ground below it by negative cloud particles attracting to positive ground particles. The forked appearance, remember, comes from the stepped leader following several different branching paths to reach the ground. The connection point is where the bright return stroke happens along the channel.

There may be several transfers of these charges that will cause the lightning strike to flicker or vary in brightness. If there is a horizontal surface wind under the storm, it can actually blow the channel along, causing the strike channels to appear along multiple parallel paths. This effect is called ribbon lightning since it looks like a series of cascading ribbons side by side.

Lightning can also travel from cloud to cloud, or within a single cloud. These strikes happen when channels connect to oppositely charged regions and charge exchange happens. The intercloud or cloud-to-cloud lightning will arc between two different cumulonimbus clouds.

The intracloud lightning travels from one region to another in the same cumulonimbus cloud. This can happen inside the cloud or along the outside. The "crawlers" or "anvil crawlers" are the intracloud strikes that travel along the outsides of the cloud. Often, they are moving from the lower negative part of the cloud to the positive part above, so the strike sees to crawl upward toward the anvil top of the cloud.

While I lived in Oklahoma, we would frequently get huge dry thunderstorms. These storms would not produce much in the way of rain but would be violently electrified. There would seem to be lightning in every direction and I would often see those crawlers moving along the clouds. The storms would be so electrified that they would appear to be glowing blue at night. A friend shared with me the experience of seeing these kinds of storms as they drove home from South Dakota, with almost constant lightning and barely any rain. It can be a powerful and humbling experience to see one of these storms in person.

Sheet lightning is where the entire cloud seems to light up from within. This occurs when there is an intracloud strike or a strike is obscured by clouds along your line of sight. Since ice crystals are very reflective, the entire cloud lights up like a white sheet hung on a laundry line.

One very dangerous type of lightning is the positive strike, also sometimes called "a bolt from the blue."[35] The positive charges on the cloud tend to gather under the cloud, which causes areas away from the cloud base to become negatively charged. Opposites still attract even over long distances, so sometimes a stepped leader from the upper positively charge part of the cloud can make its way toward the ground. It will be attracted to these negative areas that are not under the cloud base. These positive strikes can be up to ten miles away from the cloud base.

These strikes are the ones that often catch unsuspecting folks like farmers, golfers, concertgoers, or boaters unaware. They see a storm approaching, but it's still a distance away, so they feel it is safe to continue to do what they are doing. These strikes can also happen after a storm has passed. People going out to check storm

---

35.   Uman and Rakov, *Lightning*, 217.

damage could also be in danger. A good rule of thumb is, if you can hear thunder, you could be in danger of being hit by lightning.

Bead lightning, sometimes called chain lightning, is a rare form of cloud-to-ground lightning where the strike appears to break up into beads or pockets of various sizes. The smaller ones cool and fade more quickly than the larger ones. The explanation for this is not clear yet, but there are several ideas in the mix as to why this happens. Some of them have to do with the branching structure of the stepped leader, but as of now, we don't have a good answer.

Perhaps related to bead lightning is a phenomenon called ball lightning. Ball lightning is very rare, and at this time, how it is formed is not understood. It appears as a luminous sphere ranging in size from a pea to as large as a soccer ball, although larger ones have been reported. The sphere floats in the air or slowly moves about for several seconds before vanishing. The disappearance may be silent, but some have been reported as having a loud pop and sulfurous smell.

Heat lightning is simply lightning that is happening in distant storms. This is lightning of the forms described earlier, but the thunder doesn't reach our ears. The sound wave can only travel so far before it becomes too quiet for our ears to detect. Although, I have a dog I swear can hear distant storms well before they get here, and he goes on immediate alert. Heat lightning is often seen in the summer, associated with those afternoon heating thunderstorms, so its moniker comes from the fact it is warm (or hot!) outside when it is often seen.

THUNDER

When the charges flow along the discharge channel, they heat the air, causing it to expand forcefully. This is followed by rapid contraction when the air cools. This expansion and contraction creates a pressure wave that is perceived by us as sound. Thunder can be heard up to about ten miles away from the storm; after that, the sound wave has dispersed so much that it isn't strong enough to be heard by human ears. I'll use this point to be the busybody auntie and remind you, if you can hear thunder, lightning is still a potential danger!

Why does thunder rumble? Well, the fact is, if you are close enough to the lightning strike, it doesn't. In fact, if you are *very* close to the lightning strike, you may only hear a pop like an old-fashioned flashbulb, but no thunder. Very close to the strike, the thunder is traveling at supersonic speeds so our ears don't register it. As you get farther from the strike, the sounds from the upper part of the strike have to travel a longer distance to get to our ears than the sounds from the lower part. These sounds arrive at our ears at different times, so we hear a prolonged "rumble" from the thunder rather than a single loud "clap."

You can use the old farmer's trick of counting after the lightning to determine the storm's distance.[36] When you see the lightning strike, count the number of seconds that pass before you hear the thunder. Even though the speed that sound travels depends on the temperature and humidity of the air, a good rule of thumb is it takes five seconds for the sound of thunder to travel one mile. When you hear the thunder, take the number of seconds you counted and divide it by five. That tells you about how many miles away that strike was.

---

36. *English Mechanic and Mirror of Science and Art*, 235.

EXERCISE
Ceraunoscopy

Ceraunoscopy is a form of divination using thunder and lightning.[37] You can use many methods of "reading" the lightning: direction, day of the week, time of day, and so on.

You will need
- a nearby storm
- a safe observing location
- a notebook and writing instrument

Directions
This form of divination obviously requires a thunderstorm with visible lightning.

Focus for a few moments on the situation you want insight on. Make a note of the day of the week and the time of day the storm is occurring. Once you have settled in your location, make note of the order of the directions you see the lightning strike in. If lightning is in the east, that's a good omen; if it's in the west, that's a poor omen. Lightning from the north is a very bad omen indeed. South is a very good omen. Lightning occurring "out of season" in the winter is considered a powerful omen. Strangely enough, the ancient Romans believed a close lightning strike was a sign of good luck, especially when setting up a new household.[38]

Observe the lightning for as long as you wish, making notes with each strike you observe. Once the storm is

---

37. Diagram Group, *Dictionary of Unfamiliar Words*, 284.
38. Buckland, *Fortune-Telling Book*, 219.

over, look at your notes and determine how they apply to the situation you want insight on.

Exercise extension

An extension of this is using brontoscopy, which is divination using thunder. A long, loud rumble is considered a bad omen. Thunder from your left side is a bad omen, but thunder from the right is a very good omen. Thunder on different days of the week also had divinatory meanings. Thunder on a Tuesday or a Thursday could mean a good harvest. Thunder on a Sunday indicated the death of a high-ranking official. Thunder on a Saturday was a very bad sign as it indicated plague or pandemic.[39]

LIGHTNING PROTECTION

Lightning is a powerful blend of the four elements: water in the form of the rain or ice creating the charging, air providing the updraft to move the particles around and also providing the path to ground, earth absorbing the energy and charges, and the blinding fire of the heated gasses. Lightning transforms, lightning destroys, and lightning creates. If ever I needed a symbol for weather magic, lightning is it.

Lightning rods attract lightning, keeping homes safe. There are a few plants that are believed to also provide protection from lightning striking your home. Mistletoe was believed to have been planted in oak trees by lightning, so it was seen as an effective lightning deterrent if hung over doorways.[40] And here you thought it was just about the kissing!

39.   Buckland, *Fortune-Telling Book*, 167.
40.   Frazer, *Golden Bough*, 57.

Holly is another plant that is used for lightning protection, again possibly because of its association with lightning deities. Holly bushes were planted in the landscape to draw the lightning away from a dwelling. The pointed tips of the leaves served as miniature lightning rods, providing protection to the home nearby. Holly boughs were brought indoors to fashion lightning protection charms, adding an extra layer of protection from within.

Because oak was a tree favored by several lightning deities, it sometimes was seen as having a protective effect. If a family's Yule log was made of oak, it could be used during times of storms to protect the house. In lieu of the Yule log, branches or acorns could be brought inside for protective benefit. Often features in houses would be carved in the shape of acorns to take advantage of this protective effect. One popular example was the pulls or bobbins at the ends of cords like those used to raise blinds. Even today you can still find those in the shape of acorns.

Lightning-struck wood has protective and good luck lore surrounding it.[41] Often when lightning strikes a tree, it can create beautiful branching patterns in the wood called Lichtenburg figures. This wood is valued in charms for everything from good luck to fire protection.

I keep lightning-struck wood on my altar and hope to eventually find enough to make myself some magical tools. Just imagine all the energy that coursed through that wood. Whenever I have a friend who cuts down a lightning-struck tree, I always ask for some wood from it to use for magical tools: wands, runes, or anything I would use regular wood for.

The concept of lightning being drawn to the lightning rods can be used as a way of magically attracting something. I use this idea in the abstract only—*do not* go out into a thunderstorm wav-

---

41.   Weston, *Ozark Mountain Spell Book*, 50.

ing a lightning rod around! I have an antique lightning rod from an old house. I use that as a component when I need to focus or attract energy. Again, *I do this inside, not outside in the storm!* Using the same idea to connect or move energy, think about the way thunder manifests. Thunder travels out in all directions and is an effective way for me to cast a "net" of protective energy around my farm. It could also be used to send energy to a distant recipient. It could be about being heard, about cause and effect, about expansion. There are so many ways you can think of the energy work you can do with thunder once you understand the science.

ACTIVITY
Lightning Protection Grid

When I built my horse barn, I put quartz crystal points in it. Among the other magical properties, I was thinking that the points would serve as a lightning protection mechanism. I didn't have any official witchy reference for that. It is just something that felt right to me based on my understanding of the science combined with the different ideas I had read about quartz.[42] I buried them all around the perimeter of the foundation with their points facing upward. My intent was they would create a protective energetic shell around the barn and send any lightning energy into the earth. For almost twenty years that barn has stood on the hill and weathered all the lightning storms without being struck.

---

42.   Cunningham, *Earth Power*, 75; Melody and P., *Love Is in the Earth*, 503.

You will need

- enough quartz crystals to create a perimeter around whatever it is you want to protect
- sea salt
- water sufficient to cover the crystals (collected rainwater, snowmelt, or thunderstorm water)
- dried herbs to enhance protection (fresh basil and sage are great)
- a bowl large enough to hold crystals
- a towel to spread crystals out on

Directions

Time this work so you can let the bowl of crystals sit in the full moon's light.

Place your crystals in the bowl. Mix some sea salt and dried herbs into the water then carefully pour it all over the crystals. Place the bowl where the light of the full moon will hit it. Let the bowl sit all night in the moonlight, then strain off the water.

Spread the crystals out on the towel to dry; ideally, let them dry in the sunlight. The crystals will now be ready wherever you want to use them for lightning protection. You can plant them around a favorite tree, outside your home, or, like I did, in the foundation of a new building.

OTHER LIGHTNING-RELATED PHENOMENA

Some people have reported smelling a sharp, acrid smell like chlorine after a nearby lightning strike. What they are smelling is ozone.[43] Normally, oxygen pairs in the atmosphere, two oxygen atoms making up the molecule. When this bond is separated by

---

43. Probst, *Extreme Weather*, 113.

lightning, the oxygens can rebond with a third free oxygen atom and make ozone. Formation of the ozone is what creates that smell.

Saint Elmo's Fire

An unusual phenomenon that can be associated with some storms is Saint Elmo's fire, also called witch's fire. Electricity buildup in a storm causes the gasses in the air to glow. This glowing (corona discharge) typically occurs around sharp points, like the masts of ships or spires on a building. It was even reported by drovers on the cattle drives throughout the Great Plains as appearing on the tips of the Longhorns' horns.[44] Since it warned that lightning might be about to strike, it was considered a good luck sign by sailors, who named it after their patron saint. It is even mentioned in Shakespeare's *The Tempest*. "Last night I saw Saint Elmo's stars, with their glittering lanterns all at play, On the tops of the masts and the tips of the spars, And I knew we should have foul weather that day."[45]

Fulgurites

When lightning strikes the ground, it forms fulgurites. Fulgurites don't have a specific chemical makeup since they are made up of whatever happens to be in the soil at the strike location. Most soils contain some sandy particles, so those can fuse to make the shape. Other chemicals in the soil give the fulgurites their color. Iron, for example, gives the fulgurite a dark brown appearance. Copper might give a blue-green look. Barium could give a slight pinkish look to the fulgurite.

---

44. Dobie, *Longhorns*, 91.
45. Shakespeare, *Tempest*, 32.

As a very cool aside, fulgurites can be used to study prehistoric ecology and geology. Since the lightning strike preserves the soil at the time of the strike, it can be thought of as a scientific record of environmental conditions, the magnetic field of the earth, or extreme geologic activity.

There is even a field of science, paleolightning, that is focused on the study of these records.[46] How cool is that?

EXERCISE
Fulgurite Manifestation Talisman

If you are lucky enough to find a fulgurite, it would be a powerful addition to your energy work. It is the manifestation of the lightning's energy interacting with the earth element. Think about all the potential there!

There is a lot of conversation in witchy circles about the difference between amulets and talismans. According to *Encyclopaedia Britannica*, they are interchangeable.[47] Call it what you wish. I think of it as a reminder of the magical work I did that I can look at, touch, or otherwise interact with regularly.

Fulgurites are useful when you want to make major breakthroughs, bring thought into form, and alleviate distractions.[48] This exercise will guide you through making a fulgurite talisman for manifesting goals.

---

46.   Castro et al., "Lightning-Induced Weathering of Cascadian Volcanic Peaks," 116595.

47.   Britannica, "Amulet."

48.   Simmons and Ahsian, *Book of Stones*, 198; Hall, *Crystal Bible 2*, 137; Melody and P., *Love Is in the Earth*, 296.

You will need

- a fulgurite
- a fireproof cauldron or container and a suitable location to burn paper, like an outdoor firepit
- matches
- paper
- a writing instrument with nontoxic ink

Directions

Time this work when you are ready to take a big leap forward on a project or goal. A note here: fulgurites can be quite fragile, so handle them with care.

Prepare your space as you normally would—cast a circle if you wish, energetically cleanse the space, whatever your normal routine would be. With your paper and writing instrument close at hand, close your eyes and take a few deep breaths to ground and center yourself. Focus your mind on the goal of your manifestation.

After a few moments, open your eyes and take the paper and writing instrument and write out what it is you want to manifest. Be as specific as possible and add as much detail as you wish. Be clear about your goals and timeline.

When you have finished, fold the paper in half lengthwise, then turn clockwise, fold in half again, turn clockwise, fold in half a third time. Place the paper in your fireproof cauldron. Burn the paper, and as it burns, carefully pass the fulgurite through the smoke a multiple of three times. As you carefully pass the fulgurite back and forth, recite this verse three times:

In a flash, may it be
The goal I want to see
Finds a way to happen soon
May the Universe grant this boon

Visualize all the words, intent, and wishes on the paper soaking into the fulgurite. Keep passing the fulgurite through the smoke until the paper has burned.

Once the paper is finished burning, dismiss your circle or open your energetic space. Place the fulgurite on your altar or in another place where you can see it several times throughout the day. Dispose of the ashes in a compost heap or by burying them in the ground, in a plant pot—anywhere they can nurture something's growth. Visit your fulgurite daily as you wait for your goal to manifest!

You can also use the fulgurite as a snapshot of the environment at the time it was created. As you work on your manifestation, place the fulgurite on an ancestor altar to draw upon the support of your ancestors to achieve your goals.

WEATHER LORE

Most of the lore surrounding lightning couples it with the storms and thunder. Often these have to do with storms in a certain month predicting severity of winter or how fruitful the harvest will be. For example, "If it thunders on All Fools' Day, it brings good crops of corn and hay." This can be true, because a storm can herald an early start to the growing season, so more cuttings of hay could be harvested.

Another saying I especially like is "the first thunder of the year wakens all the frogs." Normally, around here, some of our noisiest frogs are the spring peepers. I hear them when we get a warm few days in winter, but they really start croaking in earnest as the temperatures get consistently warmer after Ostara, the spring equinox. Also, around this time, the changeover in the jet streams causes the atmosphere to be more unstable, and we start having thunderstorms pretty regularly. So, in a case of correlation doesn't directly equal causation, the storms and the peepers start popping up around the same time. Or maybe it does, since they both rely on the warmer temperatures these changes bring.

Sheet lightning in the night is an omen of bad weather.

This piece of lore is actually believed to be referring to heat lightning. It is from distant storms, so the sound of the thunder doesn't get heard. If there are thunderstorms at night, it is a sign that the atmosphere is unsettled and there could definitely be bad weather on the way.

When it lightnings in the west,
it doesn't lightning for nothing.

Lightning seen in the west would mean storms are potentially approaching. The lightning is portending storms in your area, so it's not for nothing!

Lightning never strikes in the same place twice.

While statistically it is unlikely places will be hit multiple times, there are some places that are hit quite frequently by lightning. Tall structures, light radio towers, cell towers, skyscrapers, and the like are struck frequently during storms and usually have a lightning protection system of some sort in them.

Myths

One practice that seems quite common is covering mirrors during a thunderstorm. While some people believe a mirror's reflective properties can attract lightning, others argue it is the silvering on the back. The fact is, lightning is not more attracted to metal than other substances. Another fear was that the reflective properties of the mirror would cause the lightning to not only be attracted to the mirror, but when it struck the mirror, it would be reflected back into the room, causing damage or harm.

A superstition that may have some merit is that oak trees are struck more frequently by lightning than are other trees. This is likely the reason an oak tree is often associated with deities aligned with lightning. This myth may have some scientific merit, although I couldn't find any formal study of this idea.

Some folks argue that the oaks are generally some of the taller trees in a forest, although I can tell you from personal experience, it isn't always the tallest tree in a group that is struck. Another idea is it is the moisture content in the sap that makes the oak more attractive to the lightning. Lastly, others believe it's the rough bark of the oak, which collects and retains more rainwater than a smooth-barked tree; that means it is more likely to be struck. Informal inquiries about lightning strikes do show that oaks are among the most commonly hit trees.[49] Maybe there's a research grant in there somewhere? I'll have to put a pin in that.

---

49. Plummer, *Lightning in Relation to Forest Fires*, 12.

One thing my grandparents always believed was that opening an umbrella inside would attract lightning. My grandmother told me it was the pointy tip on the umbrella, which would act as a lightning rod. I asked her why it didn't do the same outside. Her response was, "It makes God mad when you open it inside." I can't trace how she came up with that idea, but there are several sources that cite this going as far back as ancient Egypt, where umbrellas were protection from the sun. Opening one indoors angered Ra.[50] Plus they just take up a lot of space!

Winding It Up

Lightning is one of a storm's more terrifying and awe-inspiring phenomena. It contains a tremendous amount of energy, but its unpredictability and danger make working with it tricky. However, there are many indirect ways you can harness the energy of lightning for your desired effect. Lightning comes in so many forms; it provides us with a rich array of ways we can use it in our practice. Please use caution and common sense when working with this or any weather ally.

What are some ideas you may have to incorporate lightning into your magical work? Can you think of places it would be helpful to your practice? Even if you don't live in areas that commonly see a lot of lightning, could you use it in a visualization? Lightning is a powerful manifestation of energy. It contains power from all the elements. If treated with respect, it could be a useful and formidable magical ally.

50.   Panati, *Panati's Extraordinary Origins of Everyday Things*, 16.

Chapter 10

TORNADOS

Terrifying Storms with Powerful Energy

As a lifelong resident of Tornado Alley, I am very familiar with the awesome and terrifying power of a tornado. One of my earliest childhood memories is when we lived in Sand Springs, Oklahoma, for a short time. There was a tornado very nearby, and I remember huddling behind the couch and watching as the screen door was ripped off the hinges. Now that I am older, I figure that it was mostly because of strong thunderstorm winds and the fact that the door wasn't the sturdiest to begin with. In my child's mind though, the end of the world was upon us!

Later, as a grad student and a fresh-out-of-school professor, I lived in Oklahoma again. By now, I had a meteorology class or two under my belt, so I had a much better understanding of these violent visitors. I even took the opportunity to storm chase with some of the meteorology school students once, but our luck wasn't good (or maybe it was!), so we just did a lot of driving around and getting rained on.

One day—one very memorable, terrifying day: May 3, 1999—one of the strongest tornados ever recorded descended on the OKC (Oklahoma City) metro, and I watched the news in horror from my office as people with no understanding of what was happening drove right into its path. The F5 tornado (this storm occurred before the adoption of the EF scale), with the highest wind speeds ever recorded, crossed every major interstate in the Oklahoma City area during evening rush hour. Traffic ground to a halt, so I stayed put in my office and watched the aftermath unfold. In the following days and weeks, the stories of the survivors, the survey of the damage, and the data coming in from the scientists studying the storm burned into my brain.

What stands out to me the most from that day is I was working at a school in Edmond but lived in Norman, which meant I had to drive completely across the OKC metro area to get home. When I initially heard about the storm, I wanted to bolt for home. At 5:00 p.m., I was hustling out to the parking lot when I heard my grandpa's voice as clear as day: "Don't try it. You won't make it." It stopped me in my tracks, and after a moment of indecision, I went back to my office. The tornado, a mile wide by that point, crossed the interchange I would have passed through at pretty much the exact time I would have been there. So, thanks to Grandpa for that!

UNDERSTANDING TORNADOS

During my thirteen years in Oklahoma, I got to watch some of the top scientists in the world study some of the largest tornados in the world. From watching the weather coverage with the advent of Doppler radar tracking, it made understanding where the storm was so much clearer. When tornados spun up around OKC, there was a herd of scientists and TV weather personalities descending upon them, so tracking them was a fine art. Instead of a tornado warning being issued for an entire county as I was used to, they could tell you what intersection the storm was at! Fine-tuning of the radar signals, improvement in forecasting, and better understanding of tornado formation has all led to more precise warnings being issued. Times have certainly changed!

Even with all this, one of the biggest mysteries is meteorologists still don't completely understand why in two storms with the same conditions, one forms a tornado while the other doesn't. First off, let's allay some fears: all in all, tornados are pretty rare. Only a fraction of all thunderstorms has the potential to form a tornado. Of those, only a small fraction will actually form a tornado, and of all the tornados formed, a tiny fraction of those are the monstrous ones we see on television. Those certainly make an impact, though, don't they?

Tornados have been observed on every continent except Antarctica. Because of the unique convergence of air masses we talked about earlier, the United States sees the most tornados by far. The middle part of the United States is the most likely to have tornados, especially the larger ones, so it has been dubbed Tornado Alley. This area has the right mixture of warm, moist air encountering cold, dry air. This creates the instability that produces a wind shear that tornados need to form. While fairly rare in other areas, supercell thunderstorms are a regular occurrence in Tornado Alley, particularly in the spring.

A tornado is a column of rapidly spinning air that grows from the base of a thunderstorm. To be called a tornado, it needs to be in physical contact with the ground. While it may not look like the tornado reaches all the way to the ground, there should be evidence, such as swirling dust or debris at the base. If it is not yet in contact with the ground, it is generally classified as a funnel cloud.

Because it is associated with low pressure, most tornados north of the equator rotate counterclockwise. There are rare clockwise tornados, but those are generally weak and short lived. However, there have been some clockwise tornados associated with larger, stronger tornados. These are usually funnels that spin off the main vortex.

EXERCISE
Tornado "Wipe the Slate Clean" Visualization

I think that working with tornado energy in the abstract is the far safer route to go. Since tornados literally wipe the slate clean and disrupt existing patterns, using their energy to create a fresh start with something seems an obvious choice to me. This visualization was inspired by author Tammy Sullivan.[51]

You will need

- a small whiteboard
- whiteboard markers
- whiteboard eraser

Directions

Use this work anytime you feel you need a fresh start on a situation or you need to disrupt an energetically stagnant situation.

Prepare yourself for visualization work as you would normally do. On the whiteboard beginning near the center and spiraling outward in a counterclockwise fashion,

---

51. Sullivan, "Tornado Spell."

write out a series of words or phrases you associate with the situation you wish to change. When you have completed this, hold the whiteboard in both hands and visualize a center of rotation forming within you. See this as a counterclockwise swirl of white light. As this rotation builds, visualize it drawing even more pure white cleansing energy into it. Continue building the rotation until you see yourself surrounded by a tornado of white cleansing light.

Take the eraser in your dominant hand and see light starting to flow into it. Taking the whiteboard in your other hand, begin erasing the spiral from the outside in. Visualize all the barriers being erased, all the blockages being removed; see doors blowing open.

When you reach the center, say aloud, "The slate is clean," then flick the hand holding the eraser to cast the energy out into the universe, letting it be absorbed and recycled for another time and place.

Holding the eraser near the center of the whiteboard, begin to circle it clockwise. As you do this, see the white light of your energetic tornado weaken and dissipate. Once you have released the energy, be sure to ground yourself here to make sure any remnants of this strong, chaotic energy have returned to the universe.

Tornado Formation

The process that forms a tornado, tornadogenesis, is complex. Many parts of it are not well understood yet. Instead, I will talk about the life cycle of a typical tornado. Different sources will give different names to these stages, but I will group them as formation, maturation, and dissipation.

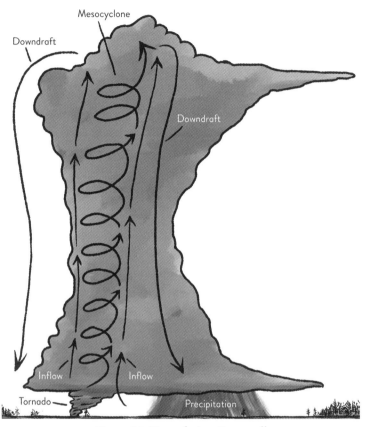

Figure 13: Tornado in a Supercell

For a tornado to form, there has to be a rotating mesocyclone in the storm. This rotation usually begins somewhere in the middle of the cumulonimbus cloud. The mechanism that kicks off this rotation is one of those areas of uncertainty in the study of tornados. Another area of uncertainty is what is responsible for causing this rotation to extend vertically through the storm. Some of the proposed causes include the wind shear and downdrafts we talked about in the thunderstorm chapter.

Whatever the cause, the rotation center can expand to reach the base of the cloud. As it lowers into the region below the cloud, it will draw in air from both the warm updraft and the cool, humid air from the downdraft. When these two air parcels meet, the moisture will condense and form a rotating wall cloud. This is also sometimes referred to as a lowering. The wall cloud is a large area of usually counterclockwise rotation. This rotation creates a low-pressure system and then draws air in from the area near the base of the cloud. This updraft, the inflow, can be very strong in large tornados. This inflow intensifies the area of low pressure and allows a smaller, more intense region of rotation to form and begin lowering to the ground. The funnel cloud isn't yet in contact with the ground. It is also sometimes called a condensation funnel since as the pressure drops, the moisture in the air condenses to form clouds in the rapidly rotating column.

The downward growth of the funnel is sometimes also called the organizing stage, since the funnel will often grow in size and strength as it descends. Once the funnel contacts the ground, the tornado is born. The maturation phase is when the tornado is actively in contact with the ground and causing its greatest amount of damage. One word of warning: not all funnel clouds are visible, since there may not be sufficient moisture to create a condensation funnel. The "tell" is the whirling cloud of debris near the base.

As the tornado weakens, it may go through a "roping out" phase where the funnel shrinks to a thin, sinuous shape. Large tornados may cycle through these phases multiple times, while weak tornados basically skip the mature phase and go straight from formation to dissipation. New tornados can form in the same supercell as older ones dissipate.

TYPES OF TORNADOS

Most tornados are funnel shaped, usually a few hundred meters or narrower where they make contact with the ground. Strong tornados, however, can form a wedge shape that is wider than it is tall. Very large tornados can be so large they can be mistaken for a low-hanging cloud.

Some of the most dangerous tornados are the multi-vortex tornados. These can be large tornadic wind fields, easily a mile wide that have smaller but still powerful suction vortices embedded in them. These vortices rotate around the central funnel, and while some are quite small, larger ones can create a large amount of damage in their own right. These are different than the satellite tornados that can develop alongside a larger tornado. They are rotating independently of the larger funnel and are not part of its wind field. The largest multi-vortex tornado recorded as of this writing is the May 31, 2013, El Reno, Oklahoma, tornado.[52] That tornado was over two miles wide at its largest, broke many of the rules of tornados, and caught even experienced storm chasers unawares. It is also the storm that killed the well-known tornado researcher Tim Samaras, his son Paul, and their friend and colleague Paul Young.[53] It was also incredibly well documented since so many researchers were following it, and there were several well-done documentaries about that storm.

A single storm can produce more than one tornado during its life cycle. These are referred to as tornado families since they originate from the same storm. Multiple tornados from a larger-scale storm system are referred to as a tornado outbreak. Outbreaks may occur over multiple days and span multiple states.

---

52. Bluestein et al., "Tornadogenesis," 2045–2066.
53. Ornes, "Predicting the Whirlwind," 35.

RECORD-BREAKING TORNADOS

The largest outbreak recorded was the 2011 Super Outbreak. Over the course of four days in April, three hundred sixty tornados were spawned from a very strong low-pressure system that traveled across much of the United States east of the Rocky Mountains. Almost half of these storms occurred in Tennessee, Alabama, and Mississippi. This southern region is where the strongest tornados occurred, with a total of five EF5- and eleven EF4-rated events.

Most tornados only stay on the ground for a short distance, maybe a few miles. The longest track storm on record is the Tri-State Tornado, which traveled across a section of Missouri, Illinois, and Indiana on March 18, 1925. This means this was a verified, unbroken track two hundred nineteen miles long where the tornado was in contact with the ground. This tornado was also the deadliest in US history, killing nearly seven hundred people.

I have already mentioned the largest tornado on record. The 2013 El Reno tornado was only on the ground for 40 minutes, but in that time grew to two and half miles wide. It also has an unofficial top wind speed of 302 miles per hour. The highest official wind speed measured is 301 miles per hour for the May 3, 1999, Bridge Creek–Moore tornado. Both tornados helped debunk some of the myths we will talk about.

By learning to read the skies, as did many of those who developed weather lore we use now, I can look for signs that a storm could produce a tornado. Notice I said *could* produce a tornado; remember that most thunderstorms don't produce tornados even if the conditions are favorable. Also, I would be remiss if I didn't say the best way to monitor tornados is to avail yourself of all the great weather apps, alert texts, weather radios, and live coverage from your local meteorologists.

EXERCISE
Storm Knife, Cutting the Storm

Because they are so dangerous and unpredictable, I *do not* recommend trying to observe a tornado directly to do any energy work. Please don't try to become the next Wicked Witch of the West—it won't end well! As with lightning, I think considering it in the abstract is the far safer option. Here, I will talk about some of the protective work I do since I live in a tornado-prone area.

One spell that seems to be ubiquitous for working against strong storms is using a blade of some sort to "cut" or "split" the storm.[54] You can ask a dozen people how they would do this working and get a dozen different answers. Here's what I recommend.

You will need
- a knife that is weather resistant (many of the granny women around here use a regular kitchen knife, but I use a special knife that was gifted to me by my Georgian Tradition "Grandmother")
- a permanent marker or wax pencil
- sea salt water or incense to cleanse

Directions
The timing of this work is when severe weather is predicted.

Cleanse your knife using your preferred method prior to doing protective work. Plan your protection marks: bindrunes, sigils, or other symbols you regard as protective. I suggest this one.

---

54. Cunningham, *Earth Power*, 46.

Figure 14: Bindrune

Scribe your protection marks on the knife blade or handle. If you want the marks to be permanent, use a marker. If you want to be able to remove the marks, use the wax pencil.

Take the knife outside and face the direction of the oncoming storms. Visualize a protective barrier around the places and people you want to protect. Holding the knife with the blade facing the storms, recite the following three times:

> *Storms be gone, be on your way*
> *No storm come here on this day*
> *Split the storm so it will go*
> *Around me and my loved ones make it so*

As you repeat this verse, slowly turn clockwise, the opposite direction that the tornado would turn, then see the storms being split and weakened. Stick the knife in the ground with the sharp edge of the blade facing the storms. Leave the knife in place until the storms pass by.

My preferred method is to take my knife outside and place it well before the storm arrives and to use the protection visualization to include friends anywhere in the path of the storms. I have also used an arrow that I will leave stuck in the ground, the idea being that the fletching on the end of the arrow splits the storm and dissipates the wind with its shape. I prefer to include a way to weaken the storm in my work since I don't want to just divert the disaster and make it someone else's bad luck.

Exercise extension

This is what I would do if I had to wrangle animals and didn't have the time to get out with the knife. I will visualize an energetic shield around my farm and around my loved ones, slowly turning clockwise, reciting the previous verse. The shield is meant to prevent the storm from crossing over my property, and the clockwise motion to weaken the winds. I see this energy as a cool color to draw the heat energy out of the air so the storm has less fuel, which also serves to weaken it.

THUNDERSTORMS THAT SPAWN TORNADOS

Remember, updrafts help fuel storms. It turns out storms with very strong updrafts are more likely to create mesocyclones and therefore produce tornados. One of the characteristics of storms with a strong updraft is convective overshoot. This means that the updraft is so strong that it "punches through" the horizontal winds that create the flattened anvil top of the cumulonimbus. There is a region where the top of the cloud appears to bubble up from the flattened area. Anytime that feature is seen, meteorologists pay extra attention to that storm cell.

Strong updrafts can also create eddies and turbulence in the cloud. This will manifest as unusually shaped mammatus clouds along the leading edge of the storm. As the name suggests, mammatus clouds are pouch shaped and hang below the anvil top in a way that resembles cow udders. They are not static features, roiling with the convective turbulence in the cloud. Again, the strong updraft could create the conditions for a mesocyclone, so mammatus clouds are a sign the storm could become tornadic.

Many people report the sky looking an eerie green color before a tornado. This phenomenon is due to the sunlight being scattered by the ice and liquid in the cloud. Once the light passes through the cloud, most of what is left is the middle of ROYGBIV, so the clouds can appear to have a greenish color. While this is a sign of a strong thunderstorm, it doesn't necessarily mean the storm could produce a tornado.

Often people will report that the tornado followed a period of calm or quiet after strong rain or large hail. This is again related to the strength of the updraft of the storm. The strong updraft creates the right environment for hail as we already talked about. Very often the way the rotation builds in the storm will put the developing tornado on the trailing side of the storm after the hail and rain core have passed by.

The mesocyclone's rotation will often appear on the radar as a fishhook-shaped feature called a hook echo. Modern radar technology uses the Doppler effect to be able to determine the direction of motion of various parts of a thunderstorm. You have experienced the Doppler effect if you have ever been stopped at a train crossing and heard what sounded like the train horn changing pitch as it passed by you. In fact, it doesn't, but because the train is moving relative to your position, sound plays a trick on your ears.

I won't go full-on physics professor here, except to say when the train is approaching you at the crossing, the sound you hear is slightly higher in pitch than the actual train horn. As the train engine passes you and moves away, the sound you hear is lower in pitch than the actual train horn. Doppler radar sends sonic pulses into a thunderstorm that get reflected back and analyzed. The pulses that come back lower in pitch indicate that part of the storm is moving away from the radar, while the higher ones indicate motion toward it.

The actual motion speed can be determined by how much shift in the sound there is. So if there is a rapidly receding section next to a rapidly advancing section of the storm, that indicates a mesocyclone has formed. If the speed is high enough, a tornado warning will be issued. Looking at this region on a radar, the rotation section will form that hook echo shape.

EXERCISE
Sweetening the Wind

Remember the aunt in *Twister*? I'm convinced she was a witch. Her yard wind art and wind chimes, I think, were there to help protect her place. I think she used the wind chimes to break up the winds and sweeten their energy. Sadly, in the movie, the house was destroyed (spoiler alert), but Aunt and the dog made it!

I use this spell not just for severe weather, but also anytime the wind is causing havoc. This could be in the winter with a bitter windchill or straight-line wind gusts. I think of this as sweet-talking the wind to calm it down a bit.

You will need
- wind chimes
- your preferred protection oil
- a permanent marker (optional)

Directions
You can do this spell anytime, but I suggest refreshing it at the beginning of the severe weather season for your area.

If desired, draw a clockwise spiral at the top of the hanger for the chimes with a marker. Apply a drop of protection oil to each tube of the chime, tracing it in a clockwise manner. Recite the following as you dress each tube with oil:

> *Sweeten, wind, don't blow so strong*
> *Strength is low, time not long*
> *Sweeten, wind, as the chimes sing*
> *Let this work fairer weather bring*

Hang your protection chimes where the wind can hit them. On days when I know the weather is due to be bumpy, I go outside and run my hands across my chimes and recite this same verse.

CRAFT
Make Your Own Windchimes

An extension of this is making your own set of wind chimes with old cutlery.

You will need

- several pieces of old cutlery (about seven—a mixture of butter knives, forks, and spoons)
- a hanger piece (I like driftwood, but you could use a one-inch dowel instead)
- small eye screws
- fishing line
- a drill with a metal bit
- safety glasses and gloves

Directions

You can make this anytime you wish. Energetically cleanse your cutlery by your preferred method. Using appropriate safety precautions (glasses and gloves), drill a hole in the handles of the pieces of cutlery.

Arrange and screw in the eye screws in a pattern you wish for your chime "tubes" on the hanging piece; remember, they need to hit each other, so don't space them too far apart. I used a spacing of about an inch and a half. If you want to test out different patterns ahead of time, make a paper template of your hanger and find the arrangement by trialing it on the template.

Use the fishing line to hang the cutlery from the hanger, varying the lengths for visual interest, but not so much that pieces can't easily hit each other. Once your chime is done, you can use the previous spell.

Using old cutlery is an interesting way to make a chime, especially old forks or butter knives since their shape could be used to disrupt the storm. You could visualize the knife cutting the storm and the tines of the fork breaking up the wind.

Even if you don't have any of these things, you can still use your words or a visualization technique to add some protective energy to your property. To me, the protection is in the intention, not the "stuff." The stuff is just there as a reminder. Magic doesn't have to be complicated or expensive to be effective!

TORNADO SEASON

Tornado season is generally considered to be spring. In some places, a second season of more likely tornadic weather occurs in the fall. This is because the unstable conditions that favor tornado formation are more likely during this transition from winter to summer and back. However, tornados can form at any time of the year. In fact, two of the most memorable tornados in my state formed during meteorological winter. One was in January of 1999 during a large tornado outbreak, with over a hundred tornados reported during the two-day outbreak. The other was the Super Tuesday tornado of February 2008, which deeply impacted my hometown. In fact, I remember clearly racing to get home ahead of that storm since I knew my elderly parents would be paying absolutely no attention to the weather. Side note, I was completely right. I blew in the door to find the weather radio screaming and my parents sitting in the den in their recliners watching the Western channel. Luckily for us, the storm had veered to the east and missed the farm.

I want to talk about the difference between tornado watches and warnings, since this is an area of confusion. A tornado watch means conditions are favorable for severe weather, including possibly tornados. In the United States, the NOAA Storm Prediction Center issues tornado watches. They are issued in advance of the weather system entering an area, often a day or more ahead of time. They cover a large area of a state or can even cover multiple states. Watches give you advanced notice to pay special attention to the weather.

Tornado warnings are an alert that danger is imminent. Tornado warnings are issued by the local NOAA National Weather Service Forecast Office. The warning is issued once a tornado has either been indicated by radar or has been reported by a storm spotter. The warning area is much smaller than the watch area but can still stretch over multiple counties.

Using Storm-Felled Wood

A dear friend of mine is a magical toolmaker. They love to use things they can find in nature, wild crafted from their property to make their wares. One of their preferred materials for making wands is storm-felled wood. Wood from a tree that was damaged in a tornado carries the energy of that storm. A wand from a tornado tree would be a powerful tool for attraction but also protection and cleansing.

THE ENHANCED FUJITA SCALE

How strong or damaging a tornado is can be determined by its rating on the Enhanced Fujita scale. The is the replacement for the original Fujita, or F, scale that was introduced in 1971 and used until 2007. The Enhanced Fujita, or EF, scale is a more accurate and discriminating scale than the original F scale. The EF scale considers a broader range of building type and types of damage to both structures and vegetation. Often tornados were underrated on the older scale because they didn't hit any structures, instead only damaging vegetation.

The range of the EF scale is from zero to five. The storms are rated based on the damage as determined by inspectors from the National Weather Service. That damage assessment is used to assign the EF rating, and then the range of wind speed is determined from that scale. Most tornados don't get direct wind measurements from storm chasers, so the EF scale is used to determine the wind speeds indirectly.

ACTIVITY
Tornado Protection Jars

Because I live on family land and because I may not be at home to access my storm knife, I wanted to make something a little more permanent for protection. I make protection jars ahead of storm season and bury them around my property line. I keep small jars from condiments for just this purpose since they don't take as much to fill and don't need that deep of a hole to bury. When you have a farm property, you've got to stretch things out!

You can do this with easy-to-find or recycled items.

You will need
- glass jars with lids large enough to accommodate your items

- elements that signify protection (old knife blades, fresh or dried lavender, oregano and parsley, iron nails, quartz crystals [to add lightning protection])
- snowmelt or water from melted ice cubes to cool off the storm
- a permanent marker

Directions

A good time to do this work is before the severe weather season in your area. That will vary depending on where you live. Your local weather service should have plenty of information readily available that you can use to figure out when this time is for you.

Clean your jars. Gather your protective items. Energetically cleanse the jars and items. Pack the items into the jars and visualize them being filled with protective energy. Pour the water over the items. Seal the jar. Take a marker and draw a clockwise spiral on the lid to unwind the storm.

When preparing to bury the jars, face the cutting edge of the blades outward from your property. As you bury the jar, you can recite the same verse used for the storm knife working or you could use this one:

Surround this place with protection true
Against storms and bolts from the blue
May the winds lose strength and pass by me
As I will, so mote it be

I replace my jars every three or four years unless the storm season has been particularly busy or I have had a near miss with a storm. I think of it like putting fresh batteries in my smoke detector regularly.

WEATHER LORE

There is no traditional European-imported weather lore that directly addresses tornados. With tornados being a rare occurrence there, no lore was attributed to them. There is, however, a significant amount of Indigenous North American mythology about tornados. This includes the Caddo story about the Coyote and Death and the Iroquois myth of Dagwanoeient, the undead flying head seen in tornados.[55] Along with those stories, misconceptions and myths about tornado behavior and safety abound.

> *A small fast-growing black cloud in violent motion*
> *seen in the tropics is called the Bull's-Eye and precedes*
> *the most terrible hurricanes.*

This is one piece of lore I found from the nineteenth century. It seems it could be applied to both tornados and hurricanes. I couldn't find an attribution for this one, but I found it mentioned in a Scottish text from 1873 and an army field signal manual from 1903.[56]

> *Tornados always travel southwest to northeast.*

Since I mentioned that the El Reno tornado broke the rules, now is an opportune moment to talk about tornado myths. The first is the one that catches some storm chasers by surprise. My

55. Hüblová, "Roles of Coyote in Native American Oral Traditions," 36; Parker, *Seneca Myths and Folk Tales.*

56. Garriott, *Weather Folk-Lore and Local Weather Signs,* 24.

entire childhood, I had it drilled into my head, both at home and at school, that tornados always travel southwest to northeast. The first rule I learned as both a scientist and a witch: there is no such thing as *always*. It is true that many storm systems move in a northeasterly direction because they are pushed along by the prevailing westerlies. But tornados can travel in any direction. The El Reno tornado traveled due south for a good portion of its early formation.

If the funnel doesn't reach the ground,
the tornado is not as strong.

Another misconception is that if the funnel doesn't appear to reach the ground, the tornado is not as strong or damaging. Not all condensation funnels appear to reach the ground even though the tornadic wind field does. Also, the funnel may not be seen because the storm becomes rain wrapped, so the rain obscures the view of the funnel.

Some areas are protected by the type of terrain they have.

A myth I heard in my childhood and when I lived in Oklahoma was that certain areas are protected by their terrain. There are various tales that tornados will not cross mountains, valleys, rivers, or lakes. There is no evidence to support this claim, and in fact there are well-documented cases of tornados crossing all these terrains.

Another version of this is that tornados will follow a river course or bounce from mountaintop to mountaintop, protecting a valley. Again, this isn't correct. There are many documented examples of tornados breaking this rule.

Tornados avoid urban areas.

While it is true that many tornados form in the open cropland areas of the Great Plains or other open areas of Tornado Alley, there is a misconstrued idea that tornados never hit urban areas. After living in Oklahoma City for thirteen years, I can verify this is false. As I'm sure residents of Birmingham, Alabama, and Joplin, Missouri, can as well. The reason big cities seem to get a pass is they take up relatively small geographic areas so are statistically less likely to be hit.

It sounds like a train.

Some people believe you can hear a tornado approaching, often comparing the sound it makes to the sound of a train. Unfortunately, this isn't always a good indicator. The "roar" comes from the winds, but often the frequency level of the sound is below the range of human hearing. It may not make a sound we can hear, although there is some evidence animals can hear it. Also, even if the sound is audible to humans, the tornado has to be far too close for comfort for us to be able to detect it.

Trailer parks attract tornados.

Tornados are not statistically more drawn to trailer parks or mobile homes regardless of what popular media would have us believe. Unfortunately, the reason this is believed to be true is because there is a disproportionate number of deaths that occur in mobile homes since they provide little protection. Add to that the morbid obsession of some media with reporting this devastation, so we hear more about tornados hitting these areas than we do other places.

WINDING IT UP

I hope this chapter gave you a healthy respect for the awesome power of a tornado and that you understand them better. As a lifelong resident of Tornado Alley, I have lived alongside them and have learned that they are going to do what they do. It is up to us to prepare as best as we can. But also, they are amazing energetic forces, and once we have a better understanding of them, we can be less fearful. I hope I have inspired you to consider using tornado energy as a magical ally. If nothing else, I hope I have given you a better understanding of them so you can coexist with them more peacefully.

Chapter 11

HURRICANES

Large-Scale Storms with All the Energy Within

Even though where I live is not directly impacted by hurricanes, they certainly have an indirect impact. Hurricanes that travel through the Gulf of Mexico often do have an impact on the weather here. Plus, I have a good many loved ones who live in hurricane-prone areas, so understanding them better is important to me.

The impact of hurricanes can be quite far-reaching in terms of flooding, winds, and environmental impacts. Hurricane damage can affect gas prices, grocery availability, and package delivery. Some of the largest hurricanes have had ripple effects far beyond where they made landfall.

As the largest type of storm, hurricanes carry vast amounts of energy: from the winds, from the phase changes, from the oceans, from the thunderstorms. All those forms of energy are available for energy work. Having all those forms of energy embedded within the hurricane gives it tremendous potential. Again, though, *exercise extreme caution if trying to work with hurricane energy directly.*

These storms are unforgiving in their destruction. Indirect work is much safer and just as effective.

Hurricane Formation

Hurricanes and typhoons are tropical cyclones. They form in the tropical regions just north (or south) of the equator. In this area, the surface water temperature averages around 80 degrees Fahrenheit, so it is a huge source of thermal energy. Because of seasonal variations, the water reaches its warmest levels during summer and early autumn. I will focus on hurricanes, the northern hemisphere storms, for purposes of this chapter, but the same ideas can be applied in the southern hemisphere.

North Atlantic hurricane season is between the beginning of June and the end of November. Northeast Pacific season runs mid-May to the end of November. This doesn't mean there can't be storms outside this window, but these timelines are when the majority of storms will occur.

Hurricanes begin their life cycle as a mass of unorganized thunderstorms slightly north of the equator. The reason they can't form at the equator is they need the Coriolis effect. The storms will organize themselves around a counterclockwise low-pressure system. Often, fluctuations in the ITCZ will create areas of low pressure that serve as the catalyst for storms to organize. Most of these fluctuation waves occur off the western coast of Africa.

Tropical Storms to Hurricane

Initially, the storm is too weak to be considered a hurricane. Most of these tropical disturbances, as they are called, never get strong enough to be considered hurricanes. There seems to be some correlation between the number of major Atlantic hurricanes and the conditions in the Sahel region of Africa. The Sahel is the transition region between the Sahara to the north and the Sudanese savannah to the south. If this region is experiencing wetter-than-normal conditions, there will be more major hurricanes during that season.

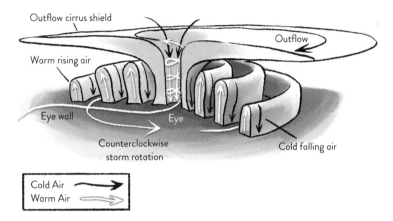

Figure 15: Hurricane Structure in the Northern Hemisphere

The formation of the hurricane doesn't just depend on the conditions at the surface, even if the surface conditions are ripe for a hurricane to form. Aloft, there has to be the ability for the storms to develop vertically and strengthen. This development can be inhibited by an inversion in trade winds, strong vertical wind shear due to strong winds aloft, or the Saharan air layer (SAL). Let's look at these conditions in more detail.

The trade wind inversion is caused by sinking warming air of the subtropical high. Remember that the subtropical high is caused by the development of the global circulation cells. The sinking warm air creates a temperature inversion aloft, adding stability to the atmosphere. This prevents the thunderstorms from developing vertically and strengthening. The strong vertical wind shear prevents the storms from effectively organizing as well as dispersing the heat and moisture aloft. This robs the storms of energy, preventing them from strengthening.

Patterns That Affect Hurricane Formation

The SAL is a mass of extremely dry continental tropical air that originates over the Sahara Desert. Pulses from the SAL emerge and move westward over the Atlantic regularly. The extreme dryness of the air and the strong winds disrupt the atmosphere, again preventing hurricanes or typhoons from forming in the Eastern Atlantic.

The big patterns of El Niño and La Niña also impact hurricane development. Remember, El Niño creates warmer-than-usual conditions off the west coast of South America. This warms the waters of the Northeast Pacific. This warming boosts the chances of Pacific hurricanes developing. During El Niño, the wind shear over the North Atlantic increases, so it acts to suppress the formation of Atlantic hurricanes. During a La Niña event, the cooler waters off South America suppress the formation of Pacific hurricanes. This same event weakens the wind shear over the Atlantic, so conditions are more favorable for hurricane formation there.

Hurricane Strengthening

As the storms organize around this low-pressure system, they can draw heat from the warm ocean waters. The larger organization begins to turn counterclockwise around the low. Because of the central low pressure, surface winds are drawn inward toward the center of the storm. These surface winds serve to add additional heat to the storm. The inward rush of air also speeds up as it approaches the center.

As the winds reach the developing storms and move vertically, they begin to cool and release their heat. The development of the thunderstorms in the hurricane is very much like what we learned about earlier. There are just many more of them and they are moving over a huge source of thermal energy. What will ultimately determine the strength of the storm is the temperature difference between the ocean surface and the tropopause. The greater this difference, or gradient, the stronger the storm becomes.

As the storms organize, the wind increases in strength. Once they reach a speed of forty miles per hour, the system is identified as a tropical storm. At this point, the storm is given a name from the year list of the World Meteorological Organization (WMO). The naming of storms began in the 1950s with the United States National Hurricane Center using the phonetic alphabet (e.g., Able, Baker, Charlie). The names were reused from year to year, which led to some confusion. Eventually the WMO took over the naming system, retiring names of storms that are particularly destructive or deadly.

Once a storm reaches a speed of seventy-four miles per hour, it is classified as a hurricane. The thunderstorms organize themselves into rain bands around the central eye. The eye is the region of lowest pressure in the storm. The strongest storms organize themselves around the eye in a structure called the eye wall.

EXERCISE
Four Corners Spell

I wanted to talk about hurricanes last because, to me, they contain many of the other types of weather energies. They are the energy smorgasbord of weather magic! So working with hurricane energy is a way to get big magic done.

I would use this spell for a situation that seemed to be immovable or unresolvable. It will dramatically shake up the energy. However, be ready: just like the hurricane, this spell has a broad-reaching impact, so make sure you understand what you are setting in motion.

You will need

- paper
- a writing instrument
- an altar cloth or other working surface that is safe to use salt and candles on
- sea salt (optional: charged in sunlight or moonlight)
- symbolic representations of rain, lightning, ocean, and wind energies
- a spell candle and candleholder (choose a color that correlates to the work you intend to do)

Directions

Try to time this work when there is an active tropical system somewhere on the planet, but if a storm's not available, needs must! Do the work!

Lightning   Wind

Ocean   Rain

Figure 16: Four Corners Layout

Place the working surface down and position your four symbols at the corners of the square. Write out your intention for this work, being as specific as possible. Include details, saying everything you need to say. Lay the paper, writing side up, in the center of your square. Draw a salt spiral on your surface starting from the outside and working inward in a counterclockwise fashion. As you pass each symbol, say one of the following verses.

For the lightning corner:

Lightning, lightning, bolt from the blue
I ask a tremendous boon of you
Lightning bright and thunder crash
May my wishes come true in a flash

For the ocean corner:

Ocean waves, ebb and flow
May you my wishes know
Currents flow from salty deep
Let your waves my wishes keep

For the wind corner:

Wind blow strong and wind blow free
I ask my wishes be granted me
Winding up the strongest gale
Do my will without fail

For the rain corner:

Rain come down, hard and strong
Keep my wishes alive so long
Energy come in flooding flow
Let my energy grow and grow

Place the candle in the candleholder and light it. Lastly, say,

Hurricane spin and hurricane blow
Let the strength of the magic grow
May my will strengthen as the gale
Let this be without fail

Let the candle burn down. Burn the paper with your wishes written on it and release the ashes in a flowing body of water.

Hurricane Movement

North Atlantic hurricanes are pushed westward by the northeast trades as they move away from Africa and head out over the open ocean. As they move, they generally strengthen because of the warm ocean waters. Because of their rate of forward motion, it takes about a week for them to cross the ocean. As they travel, because of the Coriolis effect, they creep northward. As they do, they get caught in the circulation of the subtropical high that pushes them even more northward. If they move far enough north, they will get caught in the prevailing westerlies.

In the Atlantic season, where the storm could make landfall will depend on the timing in the season. For example, in August, storms tend to reach hurricane status in the west tropical Atlantic, so these storms track westward in the Gulf of Mexico toward Texas, northwest to Florida, or parallel to the east coast. These paths change as the season wears on so that by October the hurricanes are forming farther west in the Caribbean, and they take a more northerly track, often paralleling the east coast. They can maintain hurricane status even up into eastern Canada.

In the Eastern Pacific, hurricanes form off the coast of Mexico. These hurricanes move away from land and out over the Pacific and do not often make landfall unless they happen to reach Hawaii. Sometimes, however, storms will turn northward quickly enough they will almost double back and make landfall in Mexico or Southern California.

Of course, this is only a general description of hurricane motion. The path of an individual storm can be quite erratic. The path forecasts used to model the motion of the storms are nicknamed spaghetti models. This is because the predicted tracks from various models when put onto a forecast map look like strands of spaghetti. Modern forecast models can usually predict the erratic motions at least a day or two in advance, but this is why the forecast cones get wider as they project out into the future.

Because of their counterclockwise rotation, the stronger "dirty side" of the storm is the eastern side, or the right side as you look at a forecast map. The reason this trailing edge is strong is because the direction of the rotation is in the same direction as the storm's overall motion. This causes the wind speeds to add together, causing this part of the storm to be much more destructive.

As long as the hurricane remains over the warmer open water, it has an energy supply to at least maintain its strength. If the hurricane gets over cooler water, it will begin to weaken. A change of as little as 4.5 degrees Fahrenheit can completely rob the storm of energy, causing it to start to dissipate. Also, if a storm moves over shallower water, even if it is warm, it will not have enough energy to maintain itself.

As hurricanes make landfall, they are leaving behind their warm ocean energy source. Also, frictional drag will begin to rob energy from the storm. It will slow down the storm's motion and decrease the strength of the surface winds.

HURRICANE DAMAGE

The damaging surface winds of a hurricane are only part of its bag of tricks. The surface winds on the eastern stronger side push a wall of water along with them toward land. This is the storm surge that can cause damage to beachfront properties and significant flooding. It is defined as the water level above normal high tide. In large hurricanes, the surge can be over twenty feet. Along with the flooding effect of this, the sheer destructive force of that much water can cause incredible damage. A cubic yard of water weighs an astonishing seventeen hundred pounds. This quickly puts into perspective the devastating force a storm surge can have.

Because they are composed of thunderstorms, hurricanes also have all the destructive potential a severe thunderstorm can have. This can include hail, flooding, and tornados. Even in inland areas there can be flooding, especially if the storm stalls out over a region as it loses its momentum and energy. The flip side of the rain means that often as hurricanes move inland, they can bring drought-busting rains to areas desperate for them.

Categorizing Hurricanes

Hurricanes are classified by the Saffir-Simpson Wind Scale (SSWS). The scale ranks hurricanes from Category 1 through 5 based on conditions in the storm, originally using things such as wind speed and the pressure at the central eye. Unlike with tornados, which are classified at their peak strength, hurricanes are continuously monitored and their category ranking adjusted according to conditions. The modified SSWS ranks hurricanes based solely on their wind speed.

The SSWS is used only to classify storms in the North Atlantic and Northern Pacific east of the International Date Line. Other scales are used to classify cyclone storms in other areas of the world. Anything Category 3 or stronger is considered a major hurricane by the National Hurricane Center. Don't be fooled, though; even a Category 1 storm can cause significant damage, disruptions to utility services, and flooding.

Category 5 storms can cause widespread devastation to an area. Structures sustain heavy damage or even collapse under the power of the storm. Flooding will happen in all shoreline structures, with severe damage to lower floors of multilevel buildings from rain and storm surge. Even large trees can be uprooted or snapped, but even if they stay standing, they can be debarked and stripped of foliage. Damage to roads and utilities could well make an area unlivable for months. There have been multiple Category 5 Atlantic hurricanes, but no known Category 5 hurricane has made landfall in the Eastern Pacific.

Hurricane forecasting has improved over time, so the areas of watches and warnings are much more specific now. Alert statuses are updated every six hours during an active storm. Hurricane watches are issued forty-eight hours in advance of tropical storm–force winds arriving in an area. Once the models narrow down to an area that is more certain to be struck by the storm, a hurricane warning is issued. The hope is that a warning will still give people plenty of time to secure homes or businesses and evacuate if necessary.

Hurricane winds can extend well beyond the area where the storm makes landfall; usually a significant area will be included in the warning. Landfall is defined as where the eye makes first contact with land. Because the eye wall contains the strongest storms, the strongest winds may not cross the area that is identified as the location of landfall.

Hurricane Protection Workings

My survey of friends who live in hurricane-prone areas produced a variety of suggestions for protection magic from hurricanes. Again, a popular one is using the knife to cut the storm. I could also definitely see adapting my tornado protection jar to use in a hurricane-prone area. You might add ocean water instead of fresh water or choose wood from a live oak tree since they are native to much of the Gulf Coast. Live oaks can represent safety, stability, and strength—all things that would be good for a structure to have in a hurricane.

EXERCISE
Hagstone Protection Amulet

Here is another suggestion I heard from several people: use a hagstone. Hagstones are stones that have a hole worn all the way through them. I find them frequently along the riverbanks here. According to lore, only good things can pass through the hole.

You will need
- hagstone
- ocean water
- a bowl
- a cord
- protection oil (optional)

Directions

Prepare this amulet prior to hurricane season starting.

Wash your hagstone to remove any dirt or debris. Place the hagstone in the bowl and cover it with the ocean water. Hold the bowl and gently swirl the water clockwise a multiple of three times. Recite the following as you swirl:

Storm unwind
Wind I bind
Oceans calm
Like a balm
Storm abate
Clouds deflate
Wind I bind
Storm unwind

After completing the motion a multiple of three times, remove the hagstone. If you wish, dress the stone with your favorite protection oil. Run a cord through the hole to hang the stone.

You can hang this stone near your front door as a protection amulet. Also, you could place it in your car for safety during evacuation. Prepare multiple stones and hang them from trees you want to add protection to. If you wish, take the stone outside well in advance of the hurricane's arrival and spin it by the cord in a clockwise fashion while facing the direction the storm is coming from. Recite the previous verse three times.

Please use good judgment about hurricane safety! Do not ignore evacuation orders!

Noteworthy Hurricanes

If asked, you could probably think of several notable hurricanes. Those would include names such as Katrina, Rita, Andrew, Hugo,

Sandy, and Camille. The strongest hurricane recorded in the Atlantic was Hurricane Wilma, part of the extremely active 2005 hurricane season. Strength is measured by the pressure in the storm's west central eye. Wilma formed in October of that year, reaching hurricane strength on October 18 and within twenty-four hours reaching Category 5 strength. One of the records it also set was, when it made landfall in Mexico, it dropped over sixty-four inches of rain at one location in a twenty-four-hour period.

The busiest hurricane season in recent memory for me was 2020. It took the top spot from 2005 by having thirty-one storms—fourteen named storms, eight of which became hurricanes, two of which became classified as major hurricanes. Year 2005 had fewer total storms with twenty-seven, but still had fourteen named storms, seven of which became major hurricanes with a record of four (Emily, Katrina, Rita, and Wilma) reaching Category 5 status.

Hurricane Sandy (2012), also known as Superstorm Sandy, was the largest-diameter Atlantic hurricane. Even though it was only a Category 3 at its strongest, its large size meant that when it made landfall, it impacted a large geographic area. It caused significant damage and long-lasting effects in Haiti, and even though it was a Category 1 extratropical cyclone by the time it reached the Northeast, it caused 65 billion dollars in damage. It continued up into Canada, causing another 100 million dollars in damage.[57]

There are many other storms worthy of mentioning, but I will mention only two more that have captured my imagination. Both are storms that live large in popular culture, especially on the Gulf Coast. They are Hurricane Camille and Hurricane Katrina.

Camille made landfall in Waveland, Mississippi, in August 1969. As a Category 5 storm, it is one of the strongest storms to ever strike the continental United States. The actual strength is

---

57. Britannica, "Superstorm Sandy."

only an estimate, since Camille destroyed all the wind measurement instruments in the landfall area. Sustained wind speed, which is used to determine strength, couldn't be determined, but her peak winds were measured at 175 miles per hour along the coast. The official storm surge was recorded at 24 feet, although there were some unofficial reports of a 28-foot storm surge. The intense winds of Camille caused the Mississippi River to flow backward along its length for over 100 miles.

One of the most famous stories about Camille is the ill-fated Hurricane Party at the Richelieu Apartments. According to some reports, twenty-four people held a party at the apartments in Pass Christian, Mississippi, where the eye wall made landfall. According to the lore, there was only one survivor of the party after Camille decimated the apartments. There was even a made-for-TV movie about the party. Official accounts now say there was no party, but several people did die in the apartments even though they had made all the usual hurricane preparations.

Camille did extensive damage along the Gulf Coast from Louisiana to Florida. As it moved northward, the prevailing westerlies pushed it over the Ohio Valley, where it brought much-needed drought-busting rain to Tennessee and Kentucky. However, as it moved over West Virginia and Virginia, even though it was no longer hurricane strength, the volume of rain the two states received caused flash flooding and river flooding.

Hurricane Katrina is still ranked as one of the costliest storms in United States history and also had a large number of fatalities. Katrina came on shore a few miles west of where Camille had made landfall approximately forty-six years earlier. The devastation from the "dirty side" of the storm along the Gulf Coast of Mississippi and Alabama was tremendous. Katrina had crossed Florida, weakening to tropical storm status, but when it got into the Gulf of Mexico, it essentially exploded into a Category 5 storm within forty-eight hours.

Now that I have talked about water's ability to hold heat, we can better see why this happens. In the Gulf, there is an ocean current called the Loop Current. The Loop Current is a warm current that flows northward into the Gulf of Mexico from the Yucatan Peninsula, then loops southward to Cuba. Some of the deepest layers of warm water in the Gulf are part of the Loop Current, so it provides a vast supply of stored energy for hurricanes to draw from.

Even though Katrina was a Category 3 when it made its final landfall, the hurricane winds extended over 100 miles from the eye of the storm. It also maintained hurricane strength for 150 miles inland with significant damage caused by flooding and tornados. Because of the path it traveled, every county in the state of Mississippi was declared a disaster area. Most of the structures along the coastal highway were heavily damaged if not swept away. The coastal highway system itself was severely damaged with two of the major bridges being completely destroyed. Because of the record-high storm surge, there was also severe damage to Mississippi's coast due to flooding even in inland areas.

The storm surge was as high as twenty-eight feet in some places and traveled as far as six miles inland on ground and ten or more miles on the bays and rivers. Because it subjected the city of New Orleans to prolonged hurricane conditions, this coupled with the storm surge caused massive failures in the levee systems. The flooding from these failures was the source of much of the destruction and loss of life in New Orleans.

EXERCISE
Hurricane Protection

Another form of protection magic my friends use in their hurricane prep is to write prayers or blessings for protection on the boards they use to shore up their windows. Others who have hurricane shutters described doing a regular beginning-of-hurricane-season blessing on their home. Some described going to the ocean and making offerings to keep their area safe from storms in the coming year. You might give these a try.

HOW HURRICANES BENEFIT THE ENVIRONMENT

Hurricanes are forces of great destruction, but I want to write a few words about how hurricanes can also benefit the environment. I already mentioned the effect hurricanes can have on a drought-stricken area by bringing much-needed rain. My grandpa always called them drought busters.

Red tides are a form of harmful algal blooms that occur in coastal waters. The particular species of harmful algae grow at a rapid pace and can create toxic conditions for marine life and can even affect air quality, causing dangerous conditions on land as well. Hurricanes can churn up the water, breaking up the red tide. They also oxygenate the water, allowing the ecosystem to start recovering from the red tide's impact.

Hurricanes can replenish sand and nutrients to both barrier islands and coastal areas. Granted, when I think of what hurricanes do to barrier islands, I think of the pummeling that Ship Island, off the coast of Mississippi, has taken from Gulf Coast hurricanes over the years. But, the hurricanes churn up sand and nutrients from the ocean floor and deposit them along the barrier island, replenishing the island. Without this, the barrier islands would not persist, instead eventually shrinking and disappearing back into the oceans.

The winds of the hurricanes also benefit inland vegetation. The winds can help broadcast spores and seeds farther inland than they would be able to normally go. The wind-blown matter can also carry beneficial nutrients inland. Even though the winds do damage to trees, thinning out the foliage can be helpful to the ecosystem.

One wonderfully quirky story of the wind pollinating plants is the origin story of the Ginger Gold apple.[58] Clyde and Ginger Harvey owned an orchard in Lovingston, Virginia. The flooding from Camille passing over the area caused major damage, but the Harveys salvaged as much as they could after the storm. They gathered up as many of their seedlings as they could save, including one that looked different from the others. When the tree finally matured and began producing, to their surprise, it produced a golden apple instead of a red one. This new variety was named Ginger Gold in honor of Ginger Harvey. So, the next time you are at the supermarket and find a Ginger Gold apple, remember its complicated history.

EXERCISE
Churning Up the Deep Visualization

There are so many rich possibilities for energy work within these massive storms. They contain tremendous amounts of energy they have gathered over the oceans

---

58. Jacobsen, *Apples of Uncommon Character*, 20.

that drive their organization and strengthening. Again, because of the dangerous nature of these storms, working with them directly is not a good idea. Working remotely with their energy or working with their energy in the abstract is the best way to go about this.

The hurricane contains the ocean's energetic properties within it. Think about how you can incorporate that energy into your work.

If you have an affinity to an ocean deity, working with hurricane energy might be a good choice. You could also use that energy to break up a stagnant pattern in your life and to clear the air around something in a more dramatic way.

Think about the effect of the hurricane on its environment, how it churns up things in the ocean. Its energy would be useful for churning up things that might be buried deep in our magical ocean, such as forgotten memories, talents, or connections that have been dormant or "underwater" for a long time.

WEATHER LORE

Even though there isn't much "traditional" (European) weather lore about hurricanes, there is a significant bit of lore in the areas impacted by these storms. The ancient Greeks attributed these massive storms to three children of the sky god Uranus and the earth goddess Gaia. These three sons had fifty heads and one hundred hands. After assisting Zeus in battling the Titans, the brothers were rewarded with underwater palaces. Their job is to release the dreadful force of the hurricanes from Tartarus at the command of the other gods.

African American folklore tells the story of Sis Owl as the origin of hurricanes.[59] Having left her husband to guard her food, he fell asleep and allowed it to get stolen by the other birds. Having found a source of an easy meal, the crows and jays took to stealing the meals on a regular basis. Eventually Sis Owl had enough of this. Coming out of her roosting place at sundown, she judges if the conditions are ripe and begins to flap her wings. With each flap of her wings, the winds get stronger until eventually a full-fledged hurricane is formed.

Saint Elmo's fire warns of a hurricane coming.

Now that I've talked about the cause of Saint Elmo's fire, it's pretty easy to see why this one could be considered true sometimes. The strong thunderstorms that make up the hurricane could easily cause Saint Elmo's fire to form.

If you see a waterspout in the ocean, wave a butcher knife back and forth and the spout will break up and no storm will occur.

I polled a few of my friends who live in hurricane-prone areas for local lore they knew. An often-mentioned one is using a knife to cut the storm. I decided to dig a little deeper and found one possible origin of this.

In Serbia, there are different people who serve as "hail defenders" for their towns and nearby crops.[60] Different regions have different names for these people. The *gradobranitelj* was the northwest Serbian version of this. This role was passed on from one person to another in an apprenticeship and included the use of

---

59. Harris, *Uncle Remus and His Friends*, 43.

60. Pócs and Stoikheion, "Zduhač," 386–410.

magic. When storm clouds appear, the gradobranitelj had various tools they would use, including a scythe or knife, with which they would symbolically cut the storm apart. Then often they would drive the knife's handle into the ground with the blade directed toward the oncoming storm. I don't know if that is the origin of this piece of lore, but it is a great story.

A bountiful citrus crop means no hurricanes will occur locally,
but a bountiful mango crop means a hurricane will occur locally.

In an attempt to find some science that would go along with this, the closest I could come was looking at the growing conditions for each. Both mango and citrus prefer warm temperatures and humidity. Citrus can tolerate freezing temperatures, but mangos cannot. I'm not sure if that is much of an explanation, but it is as close as I could find.

Seagull, seagull, sit on the sand;
it's never good weather when you're on land

and,

When sparrows hide under hedges or roof ledges,
a hurricane is coming.

There are several pieces of lore associated with animal behavior prior to a hurricane. Many of them are related to animals' ability to detect changes in pressure as the storm system approaches. Birds stay close to land and seek shelter when the pressure begins to drop, since the associated winds make it difficult for them to fly.

When an alligator opens his jaws with an extra-long bellow,
a hurricane is imminent.

While I couldn't find any scientific basis for this, I would say it's probably to equalize pressure in their ear canals. The pressure drop before a hurricane would be similar to the pressure drop experienced when flying, so this is possibly their way of popping their ears like I do on a plane.

Sharks swim out to deeper water just before a hurricane.

Many sharks use pressure changes to hunt by detecting vibrations in the water, so the changes in the pressure from the hurricane would certainly have an impact on them. Besides, being able to detect changes in pressure, birds often use thermals—rising pockets of warm air—to glide on. An approaching hurricane suppresses the formation of thermals.

When a cow carries its tail upright,
it is a sign of a coming hurricane.

As a cattle farmer, I had to include that one. Cattle hold their tails up when they are on alert or feel a threat. Perhaps the change in pressure due to the approaching storm is the reason.

WINDING IT UP

Because hurricanes contain so many other types of weather, you could draw from those energies as well. There is so much energy contained in these massive weather systems; the possibilities are really only limited by your imagination. Now that you understand them better, I hope you feel inspired to find a way to use hurricanes in your practice.

Conclusion

The Wheel Turns, the Weather Changes, and Cycles Begin Anew

When I first began teaching at events, it was my goal to encourage people to seek the intersection of science and magic. Those two things have never been on opposite sides of the ledger to me. From my earliest steps as a scientist and a witch, I could see connections between the two. I harbor the belief that as we understand each one better, that intersection will become clearer. Thinking about how the energies of different aspects of nature interact gives me a whole new insight into working with my magical tools.

I saw connections with the world around me that had gone unnoticed before. Mother Nature was waiting patiently for me to pay attention. What really crystallized this for me was returning to the land. I was quickly disabused of the idea that I could "master" or "defeat" the weather. Learning to work with it as a respected partner was the only way forward for me. Then as I began to understand weather better, I saw how it could enhance my magical work as well.

As I taught my students in meteorology class, I would make personal observations of the connections between the science and the magic. It is all energy; it made sense that it could be folded into my personal witchcraft. Once I understood that, I wanted to shout it from the rooftops. This book comes from that excitement and understanding. I hope you feel inspired to welcome weather as a partner in your work.

The suggestions I have made for your magical practice are in no way prescriptive. I want you to use my ideas as inspiration rather than canon. Your magical practice will be more effective if you make it personal. You may live in an apartment in the heart of the city, or you may live off the grid in a cabin in the woods. Weather is accessible to us all. Even if you live in a region where some types of weather don't occur, they are happening somewhere at some point, so that means that energy is out there literally in the air. Reach for it! Take what you learn, mix it up, and make your own concoction of practices that work for you.

REMEMBER TO BE CAUTIOUS

I will reiterate the point that having some experience for much of this work is essential. This work is powerful—weather energies are big energies! Having a good understanding of magical self-care, of using energetic "hygiene" as you complete your work, of making sure you are grounding yourself—all of these things are responsible, smart, and imperative for your well-being. If you take from Mother Nature, whether it is a bucket of snow, a shell, or a piece of lightning-struck wood, remember to give thanks for it and leave a small offering in return for the blessing of that magical gift.

Additionally, no amount of protective work can replace good old common sense. Part of magical protection work is making sure you have your emergency plans in place, making sure you have what you need for an upcoming storm, and being sensible about the dangers of weather. All this is part of weather witchery.

With all these words of warning, I don't want to discourage you from learning and exploring. There is some part of this practice that is accessible to everyone, regardless of where they are on their journey. To me, it's vital to never stop learning, exploring, and deepening my connection to nature, so even though I know a lot about the science, I am constantly learning how to extend that into my witchcraft.

WEATHER IS PART OF YOU

Weather is part of our existence regardless of where we live, from the farm to the city. It impacts our lives in innumerable ways. It seems baffling to me that we rely on our phones to tell us what is happening in the sky above our heads. The lore we have heard throughout our lives really just came from people like you and me looking up, paying careful attention to what they saw, and remembering it when they saw it the next time.

Mother Nature gives us so many opportunities to work with weather energy and weather magic. The beautiful thing about weather magic is, once you understand the science, all the tools you need are there waiting for you. The energy is in the weather— nothing else is required! I hope I have inspired you to look at how the science of weather and the magic of weather intersect to make your magical practice richer. Most of all, I hope you keep looking up!

GLOSSARY

Absorption: The process where matter takes up the energy of light shining on it.

Aeromancy: Divination using the state of the atmosphere.

Air mass: A large parcel of air that has a consistent temperature and humidity profile throughout its volume.

Altocumulus: Middle-level clouds that form in layers or patches with rounded masses in the layer.

Altostratus: Middle-level clouds that form in layers that are uniformly smooth.

Anemometer: An instrument that measures wind speed.

Anemoscopy: Divination using wind speed and direction.

Anemosomancy: See *anemoscopy.*

Animism: The belief that plants, inanimate objects and natural phenomena have a soul or divine spirit.

Atmosphere: The layers of gases that surround a planet and are held in place by gravity.

Atmospheric pressure: The force per area on surfaces exerted by the weight of the atmosphere.

Ball lightning: An unusual form of lightning that is a roughly spherical orb of electricity.

Barometer: An instrument that measures atmospheric pressure.

Bead lightning: Lightning that appears in the discharge channel like a string of beads.

Bergeron process: Producing precipitation by using ice crystals as nucleation seeds.

Big bang nucleosynthesis: The formation of the lightest elements (H, He, Li, Be, B) during the early stages of the history of the universe.

Blizzard: Severe winter weather that has high winds, creating poor visibility from blowing snow.

Boiling: The act of raising a liquid to a temperature where it turns to vapor.

Boiling point: The temperature at which boiling occurs.

Bow echo: A radar signature of a line of thunderstorms that is in a bow shape.

Brontoscopy: Divination by thunder.

Cap: Stable, dry, warm air that is layered over a mass of warm humid air, preventing it from rising to form storms.

Celsius scale: A temperature scale where there are 100 divisions between the freezing point of water (0) and the boiling point of water (100) (measured at sea level).

Centering: A practice to find calmness and balance within yourself before beginning magical or other energetic work.

Ceraunoscopy: Divinations using thunder and lightning.

Chakras: Seven centers of spiritual power in the human body.

Chaomancy: Divination by aerial, atmospheric phenomena.

Chinook wind: A warm, dry, downslope wind on the eastern side of the Rocky Mountains.

Cirrocumulus: A high-level cloud that consists of small white patches.

Cirrostratus: A high-level cloud that is very thin, composed of ice that covers the sky.

Cirrus: A high-level cloud that is composed of wispy filaments that have the appearance of hair.

Climate: The average weather over a long period in a region.

Climate change: A sustained change in the climate over a region, usually lasting for a decade or more.

Cloud: A collection of water droplets or ice crystals in the atmosphere.

Cloud form: The physical shape, appearance, and size of a cloud.

Coalescence: The merging of smaller droplets into larger ones.

Cohesion: Attraction between two adjacent parts of a solid or liquid that holds matter together.

Cold front: The boundary where a cold air mass is advancing a warm air mass.

Collision-coalescence process: A mechanism to produce precipitation by droplets hitting then merging.

Complementary colors: Colors of light that when mixed produce white light.

Condensation: Vapor changing into a liquid by releasing latent heat.

Condensation nucleus: Small particles that provide a surface for cloud droplets to collect on.

Conduction: Transfer of heat via direct contact between two materials.

Continental polar air mass: A dry low-temperature air parcel.

Continental-tropical air mass: A dry high-temperature air parcel.

Convection: Movement in gases or liquids in which warmer parts rise and cooler parts sink.

Convergence: The action where horizontal winds flow into a region.

Coriolis effect: The apparent deflection of a free-moving fluid due to the rotation of the earth.

Corona: An optical phenomenon composed of a series of concentric colored rings around the moon or sun due to cloud cover.

Density: The ratio of the mass of matter to the volume it occupies.

Deosil: Sunwise or clockwise rotation.

Deposition: The process of a vapor turning directly into a solid through the release of latent heat.

Derecho: A cluster of severe thunderstorms that have strong, straight-line winds.

Dew: Water vapor that condenses when the temperature of the air drops, usually occurring overnight.

Dewpoint: The temperature air cools to that will cause saturation so that dew forms.

Dispersion: Separation of white light into the colors of a rainbow.

Dissipating stage: The end stage of an air mass thunderstorm where downdrafts have completely blocked any updrafts.

Divergence: Horizontal winds flowing outward from a region.

Doldrum: A low-pressure, calm region near the equator.

Doppler effect: The change in the frequency of sound or light due to relative motion of the source and/or the observer.

Downburst: A strong, localized downdraft associated with severe thunderstorms.

Drought: Abnormally dry weather over a long enough time to cause an impact on agriculture and the water table.

Dust Bowl: A historical event in the early 1930s when there was severe soil erosion over the states of New Mexico, Colorado, Kansas, and Texas, causing severe loss of vegetation.

Elder (title): A person who has been elevated to the highest degree of training in a particular witchcraft tradition and in some cases is now able to become a teacher or hive off a coven. This may vary depending on the tradition.

Electromagnetic waves: Energy propagating in the form of some type of light.

El Niño effect: A westward-extending ocean warming across the eastern tropical Pacific Ocean and the associated effects on the atmosphere.

Ember Days: Days in the liturgical calendar of the Western Christian tradition that have significance for predicting weather in the coming year.

Energy: The ability of a system to do work either physically or magically.

Energy hygiene: The final step of energy work where any connections that need to be returned to the practitioner have been attended to.

Enhanced Fujita scale: A system to describe tornado severity by assessing the damage it caused.

Exosphere: The outer layer of the atmosphere.

Eye: The center of a hurricane where the winds are light and the skies can be clear.

Eye wall: The ring of strong thunderstorms that surrounds the eye of a hurricane.

Fahrenheit scale: A temperature scale where there are 180 divisions between the freezing point of water (32 degrees) and the boiling point of water (212 degrees) (measured at sea level).

Fallstreaks: Ice crystals that fall from a cloud but evaporate before reaching the ground.

Ferrel cell: The middle-latitude cell of the three-cell global wind circulation model.

Flash flood: A localized rapid rising of water, usually with little warning, following a period of heavy rain.

Flower of Life: A geometric flower pattern of interconnected circles sometimes used in systems such as sacred geometry.

Flurry: A light shower of snow.

Foehn wind: A warm, dry downslope wind in the rain shadow of a mountain range.

Fog: A cloud that sits at surface level.

Forked lightning: Cloud-to-ground lightning that has branches of heated gas.

Freeze: A winter condition where the air temperature drops below freezing for a long enough period to damage vegetation.

Freezing: A liquid transforming to a solid by releasing latent heat.

Freezing point: The temperature at which freezing occurs.

Freezing rain: Rain that falls as a liquid then flash freezes once it strikes a surface that is below freezing point.

Frost: The deposition of ice on exposed surfaces.

Fulgurite: A tube of fused sand particles formed by a lightning strike.

Funnel cloud: The funnel-shaped condensation that extends from the rotating base of a thunderstorm.

Georgian Tradition of Witchcraft: A Wiccan tradition founded in the United States in 1970 by George (Pat) Patterson.

Graupel: Ice particles that form in a cloud that are between two and five millimeters in diameter.

Grounding (magical): The process of pushing excess energy from magical work out of your being and into the ground or another object.

Gulf Stream: A warm fast-moving ocean current along the east coast of the United States.

Gust frost: A strong wind that is the boundary between the downdraft of a cold front and the warm, humid air it is overtaking.

Gyre: A large circular ocean current.

Hadley cell: The circulation cell that rises near the equator and sinks at about 30 degrees latitude.

Hailstones: Particles of ice usually formed by thunderstorms.

Heat: Thermal energy transferred between systems of different temperature.

Heat capacity: The ratio of absorbed or released heat to the corresponding change in temperature of a material.

Heat index: How hot it actually feels based on a combination of air temperature and humidity.

Heat lightning: Lightning that is seen but is too distant to hear the thunder.

High: An area of high atmospheric pressure that rotates clockwise in the northern hemisphere and counterclockwise in the southern hemisphere.

Hook echo: The characteristic Doppler radar shape of a potential tornado.

Horse latitudes: The belt of latitude around 30 degrees with little surface wind and hot, dry conditions.

Humidity: A measure of air's water vapor content.

Hurricane: A tropical cyclone with sustained winds of at least seventy-four miles per hour.

Hurricane warning: An alert that a hurricane is likely to strike an area within twenty-four hours.

Hurricane watch: An alert that a hurricane could strike an area within a few days' time.

Ice storm: A winter storm with a substantial amount of sleet, freezing rain, or freezing drizzle.

Infrared radiation: Electromagnetic waves that are longer than the wavelength of visible light.

Intention (magical): The purpose of the energy work you are about to undertake.

Intertropical convergence zone (ITCZ): The boundary between the wind systems of the northern and southern hemispheres.

Inversion: The condition of air temperature increasing with altitude.

Jet stream: Strong horizontal winds in the upper troposphere.

Katabatic wind: A downslope wind driven by gravity.

Kinetic energy: Energy of motion.

Land breeze: A coastal breeze that blows from land to sea.

La Niña: The condition that results from the eastern tropical Pacific being cooler than normal.

Lapse rate: The rate that temperature decreases with altitude.

Latent heat: The heat that is released in a phase change but doesn't change the temperature of a substance.

Lightning: An electrical discharge from a thunderstorm.

Low: A system of low pressure that rotates counterclockwise in the northern hemisphere and clockwise in the southern hemisphere.

Mammatus clouds: Pouch-shaped clouds that hang from the underside of a cumulonimbus cloud.

Maritime polar air mass: A cold, humid air mass.

Maritime tropical air mass: A warm, humid air mass.

Mesocyclone: A column of rotating air in a supercell thunderstorm.

Mesosphere: The layer of the atmosphere above the stratosphere.

Meteorology: The study of the atmosphere and the phenomena therein.

Minallagia: Magical methods of weather forecasting.

Molecule: A collection of atoms bonded by chemical forces.

Monsoon: Seasonal winds that switch directions during different times of year.

Moonbow: A rainbow created by moonlight rather than sunlight. It appears grayscale due to lower light intensity.

Mother Nature: The personification of nature as a creative and controlling force.

Mountain breeze: A wind that blows from the mountaintops down into a valley, usually at night.

Multicell thunderstorm: A convective system of storms that are in different stages of development.

Nephelomancy: Divination using clouds.

Nimbostratus: A dark gray low cloud with precipitation falling from it.

Noctilucent clouds: High clouds that are thin, bluish in appearance, and usually only seen near the poles.

Northeast trade winds: Northern hemisphere winds that flow from the northeast toward the equator.

Nucleation: The condensation of liquid around a particle.

Numerology: A divination system using numbers.

Occluded front: A complex frontal system where a cold front overruns a warm front.

Ocean conveyor belt: The global circulation current of ocean water that moves heat around the earth's oceans.

Ocean gyres: A large system of circular ocean currents formed by global wind patterns and forces created by Earth's rotation.

Omen Days: December 26–January 6. Often seen as indicators of the weather for the coming year.

Orographic lifting: Air being pushed up and over a mountain range.

Overshooting top: A convective structure on the top of a mature thunderstorm, indicating strong convection in the storm.

Ozone: A molecule of three oxygen atoms.

Ozone alert: Smog forming from the presence of excess ozone at the surface.

Ozone layer: A layer of UV-absorbing gas in the stratosphere.

Paleolightning: The study of geological and ecological records that can be determined from fulgurites.

Parcel of air: A small body of air that is an example used to explain the behavior of the air in the atmosphere.

Parhelia: Sundogs—a spot produced by ice crystals refracting light on either side of the sun.

Polar easterlies: Easterly winds near the poles.

Polar vortex: A strong winter storm that carries particularly cold air.

Pressure: Force per area.

Prevailing westerlies: Winds at the middle latitudes that blow west to east.

Radar: An instrument used to map precipitation intensity.

Radiation: Energy propagated by electromagnetic waves.

Rain: Liquid water precipitation larger than a drizzle.

Rainbow: An arc of color bands created by sunlight interacting with raindrops.

Rain shadow: A dry region on the leeward side of a mountain.

Reflection: Light directed back along its path on a surface.

Refraction: Bending of light as it passes from one material to another.

Relative humidity: The ratio of the amount of water vapor present in air to the maximum amount it can hold based on its temperature.

Return stroke: The luminous part of the lightning strike that moves upward from the ground to the cloud.

Ribbon lightning: Lightning that appears to shift horizontally due to the wind blowing the discharge channel.

ROYGBIV: A mnemonic device to remember the colors of the rainbow (red, orange, yellow, green, blue, indigo, violet).

Sacred geometry: The study of the spiritual meaning of different shapes.

Saffir-Simpson Wind Scale (SSWS): A classification system for hurricanes based on wind speed and potential damage.

Saint Elmo's fire: An electric discharge that is seen around pointed objects during a thunderstorm.

Santa Ana wind: A warm, dry wind in Southern California.

Saturation: The water vapor level has reached its maximum amount based on air temperature.

Scattering: Light deflected by small particles in the atmosphere.

Sea breeze: A coastal wind that blows inland from the ocean.

Severe thunderstorm: An intense storm capable of producing hail, flash floods, strong winds, and tornados.

Sewist: A person who sews.

Sheet lightning: Lightning that is obscured by clouds, causing the entire cloud to be illuminated.

Shooting star: A meteor heating up due to friction as it moves through the atmosphere, usually in the mesosphere.

Sleet: Winter precipitation in the form of clear pellets of ice five millimeters or smaller in size.

Snow: Ice crystals in hexagonal form.

Snow squall: A heavy shower of snow that can inhibit visibility.

Southern Oscillation: A variation in barometric pressure in the Southern Pacific Ocean.

Spirit (Divine): Broadly, a force that influences the universe. Used in this context so as to not limit the reader to a particular belief system.

Stationary front: A nonmoving frontal boundary with winds blowing parallel to the boundary.

Stepped leader: The electrons that are moving groundward from the base of a thunderstorm that will be the source of a cloud-to-ground lightning strike.

Storm surge: A rise of sea along a shore due to the winds of a hurricane.

Stratocumulus: A low-level cloud layer with lumpy masses within it.

Stratosphere: The layer of the atmosphere above the troposphere.

Stratus: A low-level cloud layer with a uniform appearance.

Sublimation: A solid changing directly to a vapor.

Sun pillar: A vertical stream of light above the setting or rising sun created by ice crystals.

Supercell thunderstorm: A severe storm that has a strong rotating updraft and can persist for several hours.

Supercooled water: Water that is still liquid at temperatures below the freezing point.

Supersaturation: The atmosphere has more water vapor than is required for saturation.

Temperature: A measure of the kinetic energy of the atoms and molecules in a substance.

Thermal conductor: A material that transfers heat easily.

Thermal insulator: A material that doesn't transfer heat easily.

Thermodynamics: The study of the motion of heat.

Thermometer: An instrument used to measure temperature.

Thermosphere: The layer of the atmosphere above the mesosphere.

Threefold law: A Wiccan principle that whatever you put out in the universe, you can expect it three times over in return.

Thunder: The sound made by the rapidly expanding air from a lightning strike.

Thunderstorm: A weather event containing lightning and thunder associated with a cumulonimbus cloud.

Tornado: A rapidly rotating column of air from a thunderstorm that has made contact with the ground.

Tornado Alley: A region of the middle of the United States where tornados frequently form.

Tornadogenesis: The mechanism that forms tornados.

Tornado outbreak: A series of tornados forming in a geographic region.

Tornado warning: An alert that indicates a tornado has been detected in an area.

Tornado watch: An alert that indicates conditions are right for the potential formation of tornados.

Total internal reflection: Light that is not able to pass through a refractive boundary but is instead reflected toward the way it came.

Tropical cyclone: A term for low-pressure storms that form in tropical regions.

Tropopause: The boundary layer between the troposphere and the stratosphere.

Troposphere: The lowest layer of Earth's atmosphere.

Turbulence: A disturbance in the flow of a fluid.

Typhoon: A hurricane that forms in the Northwestern Pacific Ocean.

Ultraviolet: Light with wavelengths longer than X-rays but shorter than visible light.

Upwelling: Rising cold water from deeper regions of the oceans toward the surface.

Valley breeze: A breeze that blows upslope from a valley due to convection.

Virga: Rain falling from a cloud that evaporates before reaching the ground.

Visibility: The greatest distance through the atmosphere at which objects can be identified with the naked eye.

Wall cloud: A rotating cloud that extends beneath a supercell thunderstorm.

Warm front: A warm air mass that replaces retreating cold air.

Water equivalent: The depth of water that would result from the melt of snow.

Water vapor: Gaseous form of water.

Weather: Condition of the atmosphere at a specific place and time.

Westerlies: Dominant west winds that blow at middle latitudes.

Widdershins: Counterclockwise motion in a magical sense.

Wind: Air moving over the earth's surface.

Windchill: The cooling combination of temperature and wind speed.

Wind shear: The rate of change of wind speed or wind direction at a given distance.

Wind sock: A fabric instrument that indicates wind direction.

Wind speed: Rate at which air moves over the surface.

Windward: The side of a mountain facing the prevailing wind.

Wind (weather) vane: An instrument that indicates wind direction.

BIBLIOGRAPHY

Anthony, Joseph, dir. *The Rainmaker*. Los Angeles: Paramount Pictures, 1956.

Bauer, Gerie. *Numerology for Beginners: Easy Guide to Love, Money, Destiny*. Woodbury, MN: Llewellyn Publications, 2000.

Behroozi, Peter, et al. "The Calming Effect of Oil on Water." *American Journal of Physics* 25, no. 5 (2007).

Berenbaum, May. *The Earwig's Tail: A Modern Bestiary of Multi-Legged Legends*. Cambridge, MA: Harvard University Press, 2009.

Bluestein, Howard B., Kyle J. Thiem, Jeffrey C. Snyder, and Jana B. Houser. "Tornadogenesis and Early Tornado Evolution in the El Reno, Oklahoma, Supercell on 31 May 2013." *Monthly Weather Review* 147, no. 6 (2019): 2045–2066.

Boeckmann, Catherine. "Weather Sayings and Their Meanings." Almanac.com, November 12, 2021. https://www.almanac.com/weather-sayings-and-their-meanings.

Bont, Jan de, dir. *Twister*. Warner Brothers, 1996.

Brewer, Debbie. *Sacred Geometry Book of History, Meanings and How to Create Them*. N.p.: Lulu.com, 2019.

Britannica, Editors of Encyclopaedia. "Amulet." Encyclopedia Britannica, accessed March 13, 2023. https://www.britannica.com/topic/amulet.

———. "Superstorm Sandy." Encyclopedia Britannica, accessed March 13, 2023. https://www.britannica.com/event/Superstorm-Sandy.

———. "Water Cycle." Encyclopedia Britannica, accessed March 28, 2023. https://www.britannica.com/science/water-cycle.

Buckland, Raymond. *The Fortune-Telling Book: The Encyclopedia of Divination and Soothsaying*. United States: Visible Ink Press, 2003.

Carmichael, Hoagy, composer. "Ole Buttermilk Sky." Lyricist Jack Brooks. Columbia, 1946.

Castro, Jonathan M., Franziska Keller, Yves Feisel, Pierre Lanari, Christoph Helo, Sebastian P. Mueller, C. Ian Schipper, and Chad Thomas. "Lightning-Induced Weathering of Cascadian Volcanic Peaks." *Earth and Planetary Science Letters* 552 (2020): 116595.

Conners, Deanna. "2023 Atlantic Hurricane Outlook and List of Names." EarthSky, February 22, 2023. https://earthsky.org/earth/how-do-hurricanes-get-their-names/.

Coulthard, Sally. *The Little Book of Snow*. United Kingdom: Head of Zeus, 2022.

Cunningham, Scott. *Earth Power: Techniques of Natural Magic*. Woodbury, MN: Llewellyn Publications, 1983.

Dai, Aiguo. "Drought Under Global Warming: A Review." *Wiley Interdisciplinary Reviews: Climate Change* 2, no. 1 (2011).

Day, Cyrus Lawrence. *Quipus and Witches' Knots: The Role of the Knot in Primitive and Ancient Culture, with a Translation and Analysis of Oribasius de Laqueis*. N.p.: University Press of Kansas, 2021.

Diagram Group. *The Dictionary of Unfamiliar Words: Over 10,000 Common and Confusing Words Explained*. United States: Skyhorse, 2008.

Dobie, J. Frank. *The Longhorns*. United Kingdom: University of Texas Press, 1980.

Dugan, Ellen. "Magic, Seven Days a Week." Llewellyn Worldwide, November 8, 2004. https://www.llewellyn.com/journal/article/710.

Dunwoody, H. H. C. *United States of America: War Department; Signal Service Notes No. 9; Weather Proverbs*. Prepared under direction of K. B. Hagen. United States: n.p., 1883.

English Mechanic and Mirror of Science and Art. United Kingdom: n.p., 1876.

Frazer, James George. *The Golden Bough: Volume 11*. N.p.: Outlook Verlag, 2020.

Garriott, Edward Bennett. *Weather Folk-Lore and Local Weather Signs*. United States: US Government Printing Office, 1903.

Gwyndaf, Robin. "Welsh Tradition-Bearers: Guidelines for the Study of World-View." *Folk Life* 32, no. 1 (1993): 77–91.

Hall, Judy. *The Crystal Bible*. United States: Walking Stick Press, 2003.

———. *The Crystal Bible 2*. United States: Walking Stick Press, 2009.

Hall, Nathan M. *Path of the Moonlit Hedge: Discovering the Magick of Animistic Witchcraft.* Woodbury, MN: Llewellyn Publications, 2023.

Hargrove, Brantley. *The Man Who Caught the Storm: The Life of Legendary Tornado Chaser Tim Samaras.* United States: Simon & Schuster, 2019.

Harris, Joel Chandler. *Uncle Remus and His Friends.* United Kingdom: Рипол Классик, 1892.

Hazen, Henry Allen. *The Origin and Value of Weather Lore.* N.p.: n.p., 1900.

Hearn, Philip D. *Hurricane Camille: Monster Storm of the Gulf Coast.* N.p.: University Press of Mississippi, 2009.

Henson, Robert., and C. Donald Ahrens. *Meteorology Today: An Introduction to Weather, Climate and the Environment.* United Kingdom: Cengage Learning, 2018.

Hüblová, Kamila. "The Roles of Coyote in Native American Oral Traditions." Departamento de Inglés y Estudios Americanos. República Checa: Masaryk University, 2018.

Humphreys, W. J. "The Murmur of the Forest and the Roar of the Mountain." *Journal of the Washington Academy of Sciences* 13, no. 4 (1923): 49–64. http://www.jstor.org/stable/24532701.

Inwards, Richard. "Sun, Moon, and Stars." Chapter in *Weather Lore: A Collection of Proverbs, Sayings, and Rules Concerning the Weather,* 47–68. Cambridge: Cambridge University Press, 2014. doi:10.1017/CBO9781139923552.004.

Jacobsen, Rowan. *Apples of Uncommon Character: Heirlooms, Modern Classics, and Little-Known Wonders.* United Kingdom: Bloomsbury USA, 2014.

Kokkinos, Savvas. *Occupied Towns/Displaced Municipalities of the Republic of Cyprus: A Brief Historical Review*. Cyprus: Committee of Cyprus Occupied Municipalities, 2012.

Krzywinski, Martin. "In Silico Flurries." Scientific American, December 23, 2017. https://blogs.scientificamerican.com /sa-visual/in-silico-flurries/.

LaNore, Steve. *Twister Tales: Unraveling Tornado Myths*. United States: Steve LaNore, 2014.

Libbrecht, Kenneth. *The Art of the Snowflake: A Photographic Album*. United States: Voyageur Press, 2007.

———. *The Little Book of Snowflakes*. United Kingdom: Voyageur Press, 2005.

Luna, Opal. *Fiber Magick: A Witch's Guide to Spellcasting with Crochet, Knotwork & Weaving*. Woodbury, MN: Llewellyn Publications, 2021.

McCartney, Eugene S. "Greek and Roman Weather Lore of the Sun and the Moon." *The Classical Weekly* 22, no. 4 (1928).

Melody, Guilbault, and Julianne P. *Love Is in the Earth: A Kaleidoscope of Crystals Update: The Reference Book Describing the Metaphysical Properties of the Mineral Kingdom*. United States: Earth-Love Publishing House, 1995.

Michelle, Heron. *Elemental Witchcraft: A Guide to Living a Magickal Life Through the Elements*. Woodbury, MN: Llewellyn Publications, 2022.

Miles, Kathryn. *Superstorm: Nine Days Inside Hurricane Sandy*. United States: Penguin Publishing Group, 2014.

Morrison, Dorothy. *The Craft: A Witch's Book of Shadows*. Woodbury, MN: Llewellyn Publications, 2001.

———. *Utterly Wicked: Curses, Hexes & Other Unsavory Notions*. United States: Willowtree Press, 2013.

Naylor, John. *Out of the Blue: A 24-Hour Skywatcher's Guide*. United Kingdom: Cambridge University Press, 2002.

Ornes, Stephen. "Predicting the Whirlwind." *Physics World* 30, no. 7 (2017).

Palm, Diana. *Mediumship Scrying & Transfiguration for Beginners: A Guide to Spirit Communication*. Woodbury, MN: Llewellyn Publications, 2017.

Palmer, Magda. *The Healing Power of Crystals: Birthstones and Their Celestial Partners*. United Kingdom: iUniverse, 2013.

Panati, Charles. *Panati's Extraordinary Origins of Everyday Things*. United States: Book Sales, 2016.

Parker, Arthur C. *Seneca Myths and Folk Tales*. N.p.: DigiCat, 2022.

Plummer, Fred G. *Lightning in Relation to Forest Fires, No. 111*. United States: US Government Printing Office, 1912.

Pócs, Éva, and Stuha Stoikheion. "Zduhač: Guardian Spirits, Weather Magicians, and Talisman Magic in the Balkans." *Magic, Ritual, and Witchcraft* 15, no. 3 (2021): 386–410. doi:10.1353 / mrw.2021.0010.

Probst, Jeff. *Extreme Weather: Weird Trivia & Unbelievable Facts to Test Your Knowledge About Storms, Climate*. United States: Penguin Young Readers Group, 2017.

Rasbold, Katrina. *Weather or Not: Two Books about the Magic of Timing and the Timing of Magic*. N.p.: CreateSpace Independent Publishing Platform, 2015.

RavenWolf, Silver. *American Folk Magick: Charms, Spells & Herbals*. Woodbury, MN: Llewellyn Publications, 1999.

Reice, Seth R. *The Silver Lining: The Benefits of Natural Disasters*. United States: Princeton University Press, 2021.

Science Reference Section. "Is the Old Adage 'Red Sky at Night, Sailor's Delight. Red Sky in Morning, Sailor's Warning' True, or Is It Just an Old Wives' Tale?" The Library of Congress, November 19, 2019. https://www.loc.gov/everyday-mysteries/meteorology-climatology/item/is-the-old-adage-red-sky-at-night-sailors-delight-red-sky-in-morning-sailors-warning-true-or-is-it-just-an-old-wives-tale/.

Shakespeare, William. *The Tempest*. United States: Doubleday, Page & Company, 1903.

Simmons, Robert, and Naisha Ahsian. *The Book of Stones, Revised Edition: Who They Are and What They Teach*. United States: North Atlantic Books, 2015.

Special Issue on the 2005 Atlantic Hurricane Season. United States: National Emergency Training Center, 2007.

Sterk, Darryl. *Indigenous Cultural Translation: A Thick Description of Seediq Bale*. United Kingdom: Taylor & Francis, 2020.

Sullivan, Tammy. "Tornado Spell." Llewellyn Worldwide, April 9, 2005. https://llewellyn.com/spell.php?spell_id=2049.

Uman, Martin A., and Vladimir A. Rakov. *Lightning: Physics and Effects*. United States: Cambridge University Press, 2007.

US Department of Commerce, National Oceanic and Atmospheric Administration. "The Global Conveyor Belt." Currents: NOAA's National Ocean Service Education. https://oceanservice.noaa.gov/education/tutorial_currents/05conveyor2.html.

———. "How Does the Ocean Affect Climate and Weather on Land?" Ocean Exploration Facts: NOAA Ocean Exploration. https://oceanexplorer.noaa.gov/facts/climate.html.

———. "How to Read 'Surface' Weather Maps." NWS JetStream. NOAA's National Weather Service, August 1, 2020. https://www.weather.gov/jetstream/wxmaps.

———. "Water Cycle." National Oceanic and Atmospheric Administration, accessed May 4, 2023. https://www.noaa.gov/education/resource-collections/freshwater/water-cycle.

———. "What Is a Supercell?" NOAA's National Weather Service, September 17, 2016. https://www.weather.gov/ama/supercell.

———. "What Is the Polar Vortex?" National Weather Service. NOAA's National Weather Service, accessed March 27, 2018. https://www.weather.gov/safety/cold-polar-vortex.

Vidor, K., V. Fleming, G. Cukor, R. Thorpe, N. Taurog, and M. LeRoy. *The Wizard of Oz*. Metro-Goldwyn-Mayer (MGM), 1939.

Wallace, John M., and Peter Victor Hobbs. *Atmospheric Science: An Introductory Survey*. Germany: Elsevier Science, 2006.

Weather Lore: A Collection of Proverbs, Sayings, and Rules Concerning the Weather. United Kingdom: W. Tweedie, 1869.

Webster, Richard. *Llewellyn's Complete Book of Divination: Your Definitive Source for Learning Predictive & Prophetic Techniques*. Woodbury, MN: Llewellyn Worldwide, 2017.

Weston, Brandon. *Ozark Mountain Spell Book: Folk Magic & Healing*. Woodbury, MN: Llewellyn Publications, 2022.

Wigington, Patti. *Badass Ancestors: Finding Your Power with Ancestral Guides*. Woodbury, MN: Llewellyn Publications, 2020.

————. "Weather Magic and Folklore." Learn Religions, accessed May 4, 2023. https://www.learnreligions.com/weather -magic-and-folklore-2562497.

Witze, A. "Earth-Sized Planet around Nearby Star Is Astronomy Dream Come True." *Nature* 536 (2016): 381–382.

Wood, Matthew D. *Lightning: Properties, Formation and Types*. United States: Nova Science Publishers, 2011.

To Write to the Author

If you wish to contact the author or would like more information about this book, please write to the author in care of Llewellyn Worldwide Ltd. and we will forward your request. Both the author and the publisher appreciate hearing from you and learning of your enjoyment of this book and how it has helped you. Llewellyn Worldwide Ltd. cannot guarantee that every letter written to the author can be answered, but all will be forwarded. Please write to:

Debra L. Burris
⅍ Llewellyn Worldwide
2143 Wooddale Drive
Woodbury, MN 55125-2989

Please enclose a self-addressed stamped envelope for reply,
or $1.00 to cover costs. If outside the U.S.A., enclose
an international postal reply coupon.

Many of Llewellyn's authors have websites with additional information and resources. For more information, please visit our website at http://www.llewellyn.com.